SOUTH AFRICAN SHORT STORIES
in English

edited by
Ellen Grünkemeier
and
Henning Marquardt

EDITION OBERKASSEL
2014

All rights reserved.
Publisher: edition oberkassel Verlag Detlef Knut, Lütticher Str. 15, 40547 Düsseldorf
Print production: SOWA Sp. z o.o., Warszawa
Text edited: Ellen Grünkemeier, Henning Marquardt
Cover images: © Ahmad Faizal Yahya | Dreamstime.com; © Navarone | Dreamstime.com; © Anthony Brown | Dreamstime.com; © Zafi123 | Dreamstime.com; © Anna Omelchenko | Dreamstime.com; © Michael Fischer | Dreamstime.com; © Steve Allen | Dreamstime.com; © Instinia Photography | Dreamstime.com

© edition oberkassel, Düsseldorf 2014
© copyright-holders of the short stories
(see Acknowledgements)
The moral right of the authors has been asserted.
No part of this book may be reprinted, reproduced or utilised in any form or by any electronic, mechanical or other means, now known or hereafter invented, including photocopying and recording, or in any information storage or retrieval system, without the permission in writing of the publishers.

www.edition-oberkassel.de
info@edition-oberkassel.de

this edition first published 2014
Printed in Europe

ISBN: 978-3-943121-80-3

A catalogue record for this book is available from the Deutsche Bibliothek within the Deutsche Nationalbibliografie; accessible online: http://dnb.ddb.de

Contents

ACKNOWLEDGEMENTS	7
INTRODUCTION Ellen Grünkemeier & Henning Marquardt	9
SEEDS A-GROWING Olive Schreiner	17
SATURDAY, SUNDAY, MONDAY William Plomer	19
MAKAPAN'S CAVES Herman Charles Bosman	31
MOB PASSION D. Can Themba	43
SUNLIGHT IN TREBIZOND STREET Alan Paton	53
DEATH OF A SON Njabulo S. Ndebele	63
LOOK-ALIKES Nadine Gordimer	75
VISIT TO THE EASTERN CAPE Antjie Krog	85
UNCLAIMED Paul Schlapobersky	91
THE PEBBLE PATH Tanya Chan-Sam	95

Acknowledgements

This book is part of our research project on the literary and cultural scenes in South Africa, which is supported by the Leibniz University of Hanover. As editors, we would like to thank Detlef Knut and the independent German publishing house *edition oberkassel* for accepting our choice of short stories. We are grateful to Riaan Oppelt and Marianna Visser – with their expertise in Afrikaans and African languages, they have helped us with some of the translations and explanations. A special thanks goes to the writers and publishers for their kind permission to reproduce the stories. While every effort has been made to acknowledge copyright-holders, we apologise in advance for any unintentional omission or error.

William Plomer, "Saturday, Sunday, Monday", by permission of Duff Hart-Davis.

Herman Charles Bosman, "Makapan's Caves", © 1998 by The Estate of Herman Charles Bosman, first edition 1947, reproduced by permission of Human & Rousseau.

D. Can Themba, "Mob Passion", © Bailey's African History Archives.

Alan Paton, "Sunlight in Trebizond Street", by permission of Alan Paton Will Trust, Ewing Trust Company Limited.

Njabulo S. Ndebele, "Death of a Son", by permission of the author.

Nadine Gordimer, "Look-Alikes", by permission of A P Watt *at* United Agents on behalf of Felix Licensing BV.

Antjie Krog, "Visit to the Eastern Cape", by permission of the author.

Paul Schlapobersky, "Unclaimed", by permission of the author.

Tanya Chan-Sam, "The Pebble Path", from Tanya Chan-Sam, *Mr Mohani and Other Stories*. Leeds: Inscribe/ Peepal Tree Press, 2008. By permission of Peepal Tree Press.

Introduction

Ellen Grünkemeier & Henning Marquardt

With its diverse peoples, languages, cultures, religions and beliefs, South Africa has a long history as a cultural crossroads. This pluralistic makeup is acknowledged in the 'New South Africa' by a redesigned multi-colour national flag and an amended constitution that recognises eleven official languages, namely Afrikaans, English, isiNdebele, isiXhosa, isiZulu, Sepedi, Sesotho, Setswana, siSwati, Tshivenda and Xitsonga. Forging a future and unique identity for itself, the country has initiated and emphasised a shift from racial oppression in the 'Old South Africa' to democracy in the 'New South Africa'. In describing the post-apartheid state, Archbishop Desmond Tutu enthusiastically introduced the term 'Rainbow Nation'. The phrases 'New South Africa' and 'Rainbow Nation', however, have met with conflicting responses; although they have been widely adopted, they have also been criticised for disregarding the racial and racist divisions that continue to shape the realities of South African society. It is these debates and ambivalences that make South Africa stand out from other former British colonies and other African countries.

Drawing on the country's rich body of creative writing, this anthology brings together ten short stories written before, during and after apartheid by nationally as well as internationally acclaimed writers. All kinds of continuities and contrasts run through these stories. Language is one of the most obvious threads of connection since all stories are in English. However, spoken primarily only by a minority of the 52 million South Africans, it is far less prevalent than African languages such as isiZulu and isiXhosa. This observation may be taken to imply that South African writing in English is of marginal interest and little consequence. However, English is actually the unparalleled language of literary production in South Africa. As a world language that opens up not only national but also international book markets, it has been of major economic relevance to the publishing industry. While this argument can explain the precedence still given to English, this prioritisation makes evident that vestiges of colonial rule have not been overcome in postcolonial South Africa. Nonetheless, several stories of this anthology draw and comment upon the country's multilingualism in that they include words or phrases from African languages or Afrikaans.

As apparent in the politics of language, South Africa is indeed culturally diverse, but it is also characterised by social and regional inequalities. The country has a long history of racism as the vast majority of South Africans were oppressed and denied political, economic, social and cultural participation. The Cape Peninsula had been inhabited by Khoi, San and Bantu-speaking peoples long before the first Europeans arrived. Yet in order to justify a claim to the territory, Europeans constructed a colonial historiography with the argument that they arrived at the Cape at about the same time as African peoples came in from the North. In 1652, the first Dutch immigrants settled at Table Bay; the British subsequently arrived in 1795 and permanently occupied the Cape from 1806 on. After the First and the Second Boer Wars (1880-1881, 1899-1902), the British established direct control over the previously Dutch colonies. In 1910, the Union of South Africa – consisting of the South African Republic, Orange Free State, Cape Colony and Natal – marked the beginning of South Africa as a political unit and an independent state within the Commonwealth.

Especially since the 1920s, Dutch and British colonial powers introduced policies of racial segregation. They used the racist ideology of 'white supremacy' to implement an unequal distribution of political, economic, administrative and legislative power in South Africa and to legitimise their own privileged position. By establishing this social hierarchy, they could control and oppress the African majority. This kind of racial discrimination was practised not only in South Africa, but also across the African continent and indeed in colonised areas around the world. Not until 1948 did South Africa begin to stand out from other colonised African countries for its drastically rigidified social divisions. The Afrikaner National Party introduced a state policy of separateness, or 'apartheid' as it is called in Afrikaans, which was designed to separate South Africans in virtually all spheres of social life on the basis of race classifications. Laws passed to implement this government policy were, among others, the Population Registration Act (1950), which classified citizens by race as white, coloured,[1] Asian or black; the Group Areas Act (1950), an attempt to physically separate these racial groups; and the Bantu Education Act (1953), which introduced an unequal educational system that bred conflict and later led to the students' protests in Soweto in June 1976. The Soweto uprising was a watershed event in the liberation struggle for years to come.

The political transition gained momentum so that today racism is no longer the basis of South Africa's state policy. White minority rule was abolished when Nelson Mandela was released from prison and the ban[2] on the African National Congress (ANC) was lifted in 1990; the first democratic elections were held in 1994. The end of the apartheid regime brought about high hopes for the future as made evident in the reference to the 'New South Africa'. The new government reworked the constitution and set up the Truth and Reconciliation Commission (TRC) to address human rights viola-

---

1 ... In the South African context, the term 'coloured' has very specific meanings. It refers to South Africans of mixed race who descended from slaves brought in from eastern and central Africa, from the indigenous Khoi and San, or from indigenous Africans and whites. The term is still widely used even though it is contentious because of underlying racial ideologies.

2 ... The apartheid government prohibited several political and black nationalist organisations (including the African National Congress, the Pan-Africanist Congress and the South African Communist Party) because they might have threatened the privileged position of white South Africans. Laws such as the Suppression of Communism Act (1950) and the Unlawful Organisations Act (1960) were the legislative basis for these prohibitions.

tions committed during apartheid.[3] It was the aim of the commission to take on the past and advance the reconstruction of society in order to build the nation's future. Yet despite these steps taken to address past abuses and to reshape the future, South Africa continues to display the legacies of white suppression during colonialism and apartheid. Differences in education, in the levels of unemployment, in professions and incomes, in housing and living conditions and in accessibility to medical care are but some markers of social inequalities in contemporary South Africa.

Literary and cultural practices are interrelated with these historical, political and social developments, conflicts and events. Literature does not simply 'mirror' its circumstances but aesthetically mediates between reality and imagination. Constructing characters, plot lines and settings, fictional texts can produce alternative realities and have a share in determining which issues do or do not receive attention. Moreover, literature allows for different, and possibly even contradictory, readings. Therefore, the literary communication process is not straightforward but involves complex activities of producing, circulating, distributing and consuming meanings. In other words: different social groups such as writers, readers, editors and publishers can construct South Africa in different ways.

In order to outline continuities, changes, fissures and trends in South African literature, this anthology encompasses short stories written before, during and after apartheid. While the phrase 'New South Africa' suggests a clear-cut break with 'Old South Africa' under apartheid, the realities of the transition in South Africa's history, politics, society, culture and literature are far more complex than the rhetoric suggests. By comparison, the introduction of the apartheid regime receives less attention as a 'turning point' since many anthol-

---

3 ... The TRC produced a report based on public hearings and on statements made to the commission, in which victims of the apartheid regime tell their stories and in which victimisers are questioned about their offences. With Archbishop Desmond Tutu as its chairman, the commission operated within the framework of Anglican Christianity.

ogies and literary histories concentrate exclusively on apartheid and post-apartheid literature. This focus shows that it has been of utmost importance to authors, readers, publishers and scholars to confront South Africa's recent past. Nonetheless, much can be gained by studying the period before 1948 because many genres, themes and issues that are central to South African literature and culture have a much longer history – oral story-telling traditions, language diversity and social hierarchies based on race, religion, class and gender are just a few examples.

To illustrate the complexity of South Africa's literary history, this anthology comprises short stories published between 1901 and 2005. This long time-span caused some practical problems because it is comparatively difficult to trace the copyright holders of stories that date from the early twentieth century but are not yet part of the public domain. We tried to obtain permission to reproduce Sarah Gertrude Millin's "Pumpkins" (1926)[4] and Rolfes Dhlomo's "Murder on the Mine Dumps" (1930)[5] but could not find out which publishing house, trust or family member of the deceased author controls the intellectual property rights. The same holds true for Peter Abrahams' "Hatred" (1942)[6] and Ezekiel Mphahlele's "Down the

---

4 ... Millin's story was first published in the South African literary magazine *Voorslag* (Afrikaans for "Whiplash"), founded by Roy Campbell, William Plomer and Laurens van der Post. Challenging the racist norms and attitudes that were dominant among white South Africans, the magazine met with public critique and the editors eventually left the country. By focusing on the procedure of growing vegetables, "Pumpkins" explores a maid's relations to her mistress and to her husband.

5 ... "Murder on the Mine Dumps" was first published in *The Sjambok*, a South African weekly literary magazine edited by Stephen Black. In 1975, the story was re-issued together with some other short fiction by Dhlomo in *English in Africa*. Following the popular "Jim comes to Jo'burg"-motif, the story comments on class struggles, crime, race and ethnicity in the rapidly industrialising and urbanising South Africa of the 1920s.

6 ... "Hatred" was published in Abrahams' first collection of short stories *Dark Testament* (1942). The elderly Jewish character Isaac, who emigrated to South Africa

Quiet Street" (1956).[7] While all of these stories would have made a welcome contribution to the anthology, we still put together a representative collection that showcases South African literature.

The stories are arranged in chronological order, beginning with "Seeds A-Growing" (1901) by OLIVE SCHREINER. Written and set in 1901 during the Second Boer War, the story actually predates South Africa as a colonial political entity since the Union of South Africa was not formed until 1910. In keeping with this context, the story addresses the power relations between the Boers, the British and the Africans as well as related questions concerning violence, justice and freedom. On the one hand, the story refers to this specific time and place; on the other, it creates a surreal atmosphere because it features a dialogue between the first-person narrator and the Spirit of Freedom. WILLIAM PLOMER's "Saturday, Sunday, Monday" (1927) is equally concerned with hierarchies in a rural community. Its character constellation is structured by social categories of difference, especially by gender, race and class. Moreover, power and social status are defined by land ownership and access to water. "Makapan's Caves" (1930) by HERMAN CHARLES BOSMAN partakes of oral traditions as it is narrated by Oom Schalk Lourens, the story-telling character for whom Bosman's stories are famous. Both the setting and the characters' names indicate that the story is based upon an historical incident in 1854, namely a conflict between Voortrekkers[8] and Ndebele men led by Makapan. While this character constellation might read as if the story subscribed to racist prejudices, it actually challenges

---

because of religious persecution in 'the Old Country', also encounters anti-Semitic prejudices in the Boer community.

7 ... "Down the Quiet Street" is one of the short stories that Mphahlele published in the *Drum* magazine in the 1950s. The title refers to the setting in Nadia Street, where Constable Tefo comes across a sham funeral procession in which the coffin actually transports liquor bottles. The story mockingly explores everyday life under prohibition.

8 ... Voortrekkers "pioneers" (Afrikaans), in mass migration movements in the mid-nineteenth century, Boers left the Cape Colony that was controlled by the British and moved into the interior of today's South Africa.

the simplistic dichotomies of 'Europeans vs. Africans', 'good vs. evil' or 'right vs. wrong'. D. Can Themba's "Mob Passion" (1953) also goes beyond the common focus on "white vs. black" by exploring conflicts among blacks of different ethnic groups. Presenting Linga and Mapula as lovers from rival groups, he transfers the setup of Shakespeare's *Romeo and Juliet* to the violence between Basotho and Nguni peoples in Newclare. As the prize-winning entry of a short story competition, Themba's story was published in *Drum*, an influential South African magazine that was established in the 1950s and targeted primarily at urban black communities.[9] The living conditions and power relations during apartheid are the central topics of the two stories by A. Paton and N. S. Ndebele. The protagonist of Alan Paton's "Sunlight in Trebizond Street" (1966) is detained by the police because he is a member of the anti-apartheid movement. However, his 'double life' does not only concern his political involvement but also his secret relationship with a woman. Compared to the policemen, the prisoner is clearly oppressed and rendered powerless. Since the story is written from the limited perspective of the prisoner as a first-person narrator, the reader is also not in a privileged position to "make sense" of the policemen's apparently arbitrary decisions and actions. Exploring the violence and power of the police, Njabulo S. Ndebele's "Death of a Son" (1987) focuses on parents whose son was killed during a police raid in the township.[10] With the mother as the psychological centre of orientation, the story filters events through her perspective, thus foregrounding the impact apartheid has on relationships and private lives of black South Africans. Nadine Gordimer's "Look-Alikes" (2003) draws attention to the social hierarchies that prevail in post-apartheid South Africa. Set on a university campus, the story sets apart 'us'

---

9 ... The magazine was an important platform not only for D. Can Themba but also for other writers like Ezekiel Mphahlele, Henry Nxumalo and Casey Motsisi.

10 ... Following the Group Areas Act, townships are urban and usually under-privileged areas on the outskirts of towns and cities which the apartheid government set aside for black, coloured or Asian populations. Soweto and Khayelitsha are two of the largest and best-known examples.

(students) from 'them' (homeless people who 'intrude' on campus). Yet in keeping with the title "Look-Alikes", this clear-cut division is blurred in the course of the story when the narrator uses a broad repertoire of techniques to represent the students' consciousness and perception of the events. A different kind of social hierarchy is examined in Antjie Krog's "Visit to the Eastern Cape" (2004). Exploring the accessibility and quality of medical care, the story describes a visit to an under-resourced and under-staffed hospital in the Eastern Cape in which AIDS-related diseases are the most common causes of death. Judging by the title, these deprived conditions can be read as a metonymy for deficient medical care in the country's rural areas. The story's Bangladeshi doctor, however, points out that 'limitations are relative' because the situation in South Africa is better than in western Zambia where he worked before. Paul Schlapobersky also presents HIV/AIDS as one of the challenges in the "New South Africa". With a street photographer as its protagonist, "Unclaimed" (2004) touches upon several topics including HIV/AIDS, crime, violence, accidents, poverty and migration. Although South Africa is one of the countries in the world most affected by the virus, the story does not focus exclusively on the epidemic, but draws attention to various aspects that are part and parcel of everyday life in Johannesburg. Tanya Chan-Sam's "The Pebble Path" (2005) acknowledges the geographical, botanical and cultural variety of South Africa by describing how the two main characters Emelda and Rajesh drive from Cape Town to Klein Vallei. Although they prepare a court case against a school master who abused his position to molest and rape pupils, the story does not so much explore the crime as such but rather the community's ways of coping with it. In the context of 'New South Africa', this interplay of legal and emotional responses also brings to mind the methods and aims of the Truth and Reconciliation Commission.

With its choice of texts that brings together short stories from pre-apartheid, apartheid and post-apartheid times, this anthology pays tribute to South Africa's rich literary history and provides insight into its central formal aspects, themes and issues.

Seeds A-Growing

Olive Schreiner

I sat alone on the kopje[11] side; at my feet were the purple fig-blossoms, and the yellow dandelion flowers were closing for the night. The sun was almost sinking; above him in the west the clouds were beginning to form a band of gold. The cranes were already beginning to fly homeward in long straight lines. I leaned my head against the rock upon the kopje, and I think I slept.

Then it seemed that in the sky above me moved a great white figure, with wings outstretched.

And I called, "Who and what are you, great white Spirit?"

And the Spirit answered, "I am the Spirit of Freedom!"

And I cried, "What do you do here, in this sad land, where no freedom is?"

And he answered me, "I am watching my seeds a-sowing."

And I said, "What is there a-sowing here? Our cornfields are down-trodden; at day the flames from burning farm-houses rise into the sky, and at night the stars look down on homeless women and young children. Here the walls have ears; we look round to see if no man is following us to listen to the very beating of our hearts. What place is left for you here?"

And he said, "I have watched my seeds a-sowing. At the foot of every scaffold which rises in town or village, on every spot in the barren veld[12] where men with hands tied and eyes blindfolded are led

---

11 ... small hill or mound commonly found in the South African *veld* (Afrikaans), also *koppie*

12 ... South African landscape, flat or hilly, usually covered in grass and with few trees (South African English)

out to meet death, as the ropes are drawn and the foreign bullets fly, I count the blood drops a-falling; and I know that my seed is sown. I leave you now, and for a while you shall know me no more; but the day will come when I will return and gather in my harvest."

And I cried, "Great Spirit, when shall that time be?"

But his wings were spread, and it seemed they covered all the sky as he passed.

And I cried, "Spirit, beware, lest even in the sky they shoot up at you and you be killed for ever in this strange sad land."

But he cried as he fled from me, "I cannot die! … *Mors janua vitae!*"[13]

And I started up. I saw no spirit, but the sun was sinking. The west was gold and crimson. The last line of cranes with their heads stretched forward and their wings outspread were flying homeward. I heard their long, strange cry.

I glanced around me on the kopje, fearing one holding by English gold might have followed me. But the kopje was silent. As I passed back into the village, the barbed-wire gates were not yet closed; only the dark-skinned guards scowled at me as I passed them with their rifles at the gate, and armed white men jeered as I went by them; but not one of them knew that I had been speaking with their great enemy on the kopje!

Hanover, October 25, 1901.

---

13 … Death is the gate to life. (Latin)

Saturday, Sunday, Monday

William Plomer

Saturday

When people heard that Lena was going to live on her sister's farm they said:

"Now you'll see sparks! Can't you see them living together, these two, I don't think! I can see old Piet having a nice quiet time playing peacemaker." Within a week of her arrival Lena had said to Maud:

"You are an old cow. Look at the way you just let Piet have his own way in everything. You're just spoiling him. Why don't you put your foot down? Do you like being treated as if you were a cow? Heavens, if I wanted to be a cow I'd just stick a pair of horns on my head and moo." The truth, as usual, was unpalatable, and the two sisters had a scene.

Piet quickly developed a sly, sneaking regard for Lena, in whom he saw an independence and a vivacity that he missed in his wife, but he was afraid to reckon with his own feelings, and his thwarted lustfulness began to express itself in an annoying habit of teasing. He seemed, in his conversations with Lena, to amble and flap all round his feelings, lightly-awkwardly like a secretary-bird, afraid to attack and only making occasional jabs with its beak.

Sometimes she used to look at him pertly without saying anything, and he became more and more tormented by her mocking smile and straying hair, by the agility of her body, and by her liveliness.

"I saw Jenson this morning," he said one Saturday at lunch. "He says they're coming over to-morrow. He's bringing his brother too."

"His brother?" said Lena. "What's he like?"

"A good match for you."

"What, Jenson's brother!"

"Why not? He's a nice young chap, and we should have half the district in the family then."

"Ach, Piet, you think of nothing but land and making matches."

"I want to see you settled down."

"Do you, indeed?"

"But you don't seem to know much about men." He grinned, showing his teeth stained with pipe-smoke.

"I shan't get you to teach me," said Lena. Her face was flushed.

"You may be soft about old men, but if you'll take my advice—"

"I should be sorry to take your advice about anything!"

"You may be glad of it some day, my chicken. As I was saying, if you'll take my advice you won't be nasty to the young men, or you'll get left. You'll be an old maid yet."

"Do stop teasing her, Piet," said Maud.

"You don't call that teasing!" said Lena.

"Well, well, this won't buy the baby a new frock," said Piet, pushing his chair back from the table. "I must get on with the job."

Lena was so irritated by the shape of his hands that she got up and left the table.

"D'you know what's wrong with her?" said Piet, watching her go. "She hasn't got enough work to do, that's what's wrong with her. Make her do more in the house."

He picked up his hat discoloured with sweat, and went out of the house into the brilliant sunshine.

***

At supper-time the lamp smoked, and the tea had been made with water that wasn't boiling. Piet smelt of tar and his hands were stained.

He talked until his monologue became a soliloquy about the work on the farm.

"You girls are very quiet to-night," he said bigamously.

Lena looked at him brightly without answering. But Maud was in tumult. She couldn't, as it were, lay hands on a single one of her emotions. They tormented her like internal pains that you want to catch hold of with your fingers but can't touch, because they can only be got at with medicines.

"I'm tired, dear," she said, without even the enthusiasm of fatigue.

"What, has baby been giving you trouble? Or that girl in the kitchen? Tell me if that Annie gives you trouble again; I'll settle her, I'll give her something to remember me by."

"O she's all right now," said Maud, "since she got that hiding. It isn't that."

"What isn't that?"

"I'm just tired, that's all."

But she felt ill with choked resentment.

Sunday

Although they used to come quite often, Maud was so taken this time by the idea of the Jensons' coming that she didn't know what to do. She dressed herself up, and hurried in and out at different doors. She also kept nagging at Lena, who had put a red Barberton-daisy in her hair and was smiling with her little mobile mouth. As the car came up to the door Maud exclaimed:

"Quick, take that thing out of your hair!"

"Why?"

"Take it out!"

"It's too late."

Maud was too much aware of the contrast between herself and Lena as she watched Mrs Jenson getting out of the car.

Mrs Jenson was one of those women who always feel naked if they are not wearing an apron. Now she was blinking in the sunlight, and standing awkwardly in her black shoes owing to the fact that her peculiar gait had worn down and rounded off the outside edges of her heels. As she turned, her only ornament came into view, a comb that held up, just under her hat, some of her back hair, the rest of which curled over on her neck with the depressing appearance of dust that has drifted into some neglected corner no brush can reach. She turned to walk up the steps with Maud, and folded her parasol, and shadow fell like a shutter down her back and Maud's as they entered the verandah.

Simply by following after with the two men, Lena was beginning to lay waste a whole convention: because when South Africans visit each other in the country the sexes are nearly always segregated – a woman who talks to men is immoral, a man who talks to women is a 'ladies' man'. Lena was walking up with Jenson's brother, Piet and Jenson behind them.

"The animals went in two by two," she said, winking at Jenson over her shoulder. She liked Jenson, who admired her with the greatest caution on account of his wife. He returned her wink. Piet's face in the white sunlight looked lined and covetous, his eyes strenuously clear, as though they were searching an expanse of open veld,[14] in the hope of coming soon upon further and further vistas. So many morgen,[15] so many joys.

Jenson's brother's name was Jock, and his laughing mouth was full of chewing-gum. He had a permanent dazzle in his face, as if he never ceased being surprised at his own good health and good temper.

---

14 ... South African landscape, flat or hilly, usually covered in grass and with few trees (South African English)

15 ... morning (Afrikaans), also a land measure, i.e. about the amount of land that can be ploughed in a morning

They all sat down to tea in the deep shade of the verandah, on the parapet of which there were elaborate green-and-white tins containing ferns and plants with red and variegated leaves. They sat round the table, which was covered by a cloth made entirely of lace.

Maud, who had always accepted without a struggle all the colonial customs and repressions, under whose influence she had been brought up, began pouring out the tea with puzzled concentration and slow dexterity, conscious of little but the painful effort of impressing the party with her gentility. Jenson was handing plates of little cakes of many shapes and sizes. Some had scalloped edges, others were covered with pink icing, which had seemed to Maud a suitable colour for the occasion: it was as though by having his tongue confused with pink icing Jenson might be persuaded to allow Piet certain desired concessions, grazing rights and water rights in further and yet further prairies of parched and rolling plain.

They were all sitting so near together that Jenson hardly had to move his feet; he just bowed from the waist, a plate lying flat on the palm of each hand. He bowed slowly up and down with movements as of some vast and graceful insect, first on this side, then on that side, so that Lena was moved to remark to his wife:

"Doesn't Mr Jenson do it beautifully?"

Mrs Jenson drew herself up another half-inch.

"He's quite the ladies' man this afternoon," she said, with as much pride as spite.

She had only taken one bite out of the tiny piece of bread-and-butter on her plate, and her little finger was like a hook on which to hang a whole system of genteel behaviour. Lena, noticing a cleft in the tip of Mrs Jenson's nose, turned to Jock:

"Do have one of the ones with cherries on top," she said. "When I made them I put a double quantity of sugar in."

Maud would have liked her guests to think that a servant had prepared the food. She knew they would guess now that she and Lena had been cooking all the morning.

Jock ate four of the buns with cherries on top. "What are those dark trees at the bottom of the garden?" he asked, beaming and chewing.

"*Cupressus lusitanica*," said Piet. It was all the Latin he knew.

"Come on," said Lena, "let's go and look at them."

She and Jock went down the steps together. Before they got to the trees they were arm in arm.

Maud and Piet and Mrs Jenson were left as silent as ruins after a cyclone. Only Jenson stood firm, and he smiled. Piet, in an attempt to recover the lost proprieties, took him off to look at a pigsty.

***

That night Lena went to bed early. She wanted to think about young Jenson, who had promised to come to-morrow afternoon and take her out for a ride.

When she was in her nightdress she lighted a cigarette. Then she took out of a drawer a tin box containing a broken necklace of green glass beads which she wanted to wear next day. She sat on the bed, her short strong legs hanging over the side, and the box of beads lying open in her lap.

There was a knock at the door, and Maud came in just as Lena was thoughtfully killing her cigarette.

"You're not *smoking*," said Maud with concentrated passion.

Lena looked up. Her sister was wearing a long plain dressing-gown which flapped round her feet, and made her seem taller than she really was. So long and soft and angry, she stood there like a spectre out of a forgotten time. Indeed, although under thirty, she belonged to a period that seems to have come to an end.

Lena began crooning to herself:

"Half a woman and half a tree,
She can't change it,
She can't change it,

*So we'll chop her up for firewood
In the sweet by and by."*

She sucked a thread, slipped it through a bead, which she held between her fingers as delicately as a grape, and then began casually tying a knot.

"Hullo," she said to Maud, without looking up.

"Lena," said Maud with false quietness (she was almost suffocated with rage), "what would mother have said?"

"What about?"

"What about? You know what about! About the way you behaved this afternoon!"

"Me?"

"You! What would mother have said?"

"I don't see what mother's got to do with it. When people are dead—"

Maud began to cry.

"O dry up," said Lena, getting into bed.

"You little beast," cried Maud in a broken voice, "you devil! How *can* you be so wicked, so ungrateful, *wicked* – a Kaffir[16] woman wouldn't behave the way you behave – you may treat me like this, but don't speak – I can't bear it – don't ever speak slightingly of mother again! How you *dare* even think of it! And then to say it to *me*—"

Maud saw the room dancing through her tears, and Lena being tossed in the bed as if it was a boat.

"Tell me what I've done," said Lena, "if it amuses you."

"*Tula!*"[17] said Maud harshly, as she would say to a native servant she wanted to silence. "How you *can*—"

"This isn't the kitchen," said Lena.

---

16 … very offensive term for black South Africans

17 … Shut up! Be quiet! (isiXhosa and isiZulu)

"Kitchen! You talk to me of kitchens! *My* kitchen! A lot you've ever done in my kitchen! You're a little butterfly, aren't you? A little butterfly!" she repeated scornfully. "O no, in the upper ten we never go into our kitchens, do we?"

"Never," said Lena.

"O *no*! Here you live, you're *content* to live, in *my* house, *my* house, doing no work, living on Piet's labour, and then you can't even be polite to him; day in, day out, fine or wet, *he* has to go out and work, and here you come and we treat you like a queen and what thanks do *I* get? Eh? Tell me, what thanks, I say? You taunt me with kitchens, you snake! You lie in bed and thread your dirty beads like a fine lady and insult my friends, *my* friends, while I can go hang. Selfish, you're worse than that—"

"Insult your friends?"

"Look at the way you treated Mrs Jenson! She'll never come here again! You know Piet wants to get grazing rights from him, and land, and you can't even be polite. No, I shouldn't think Mr Jenson's ever been so insulted! You talked like a bad, fast woman! What would poor, poor dad have said?"

"First it's poor, poor mother, and then it's poor, poor dad, and then it's poor, poor grazing rights. Really, Maud, you don't know what you're talking about."

"You mock at your parents! You mock at God! You mock at my husband, *my* husband! You mock at me! Wait! Wait!! I'll show you whose house this is—"

Lena was frightened. Her heart was beating at a terrible pace, her lips were dry, and her tongue seemed to stick to the roof of her mouth. It was all she could do to control herself.

She affected to yawn.

"My dear Maud, if you can't talk quietly, why not go to bed?" Her voice trembled. "Good night." She turned over and pretended she was going to sleep.

"Bed! bed!" Maud's voice vibrated so that she couldn't utter another word.

She wanted to strike her sister, and lifted her hand, but let it fall again. She wanted to point out that Piet was her husband, but all she could do, trembling and with set lips, was to walk slowly out of the room.

Monday

Maud used to sleep in the afternoon. Before getting ready for her ride Lena wanted to tell her she would be out for tea, so she went and knocked at her sister's door. There was no answer, so she looked in. The blinds were down, and Maud was still asleep. Lena closed the door softly, and went back to her own room.

Having achieved, at the end of an hour, that look of unstudied disorder which was part of her charm, she sauntered out, and stood waiting at the gate for young Jenson. After some time she began strolling up and down outside, and, as she walked, impatiently tapped her shoes with a little riding-switch she carried.

Meanwhile Maud had got up, and happening to go out on the verandah to see if the plants had been watered she noticed a figure in blue sauntering down the road beyond the gate with a light and youthful step, the figure of Lena. She would have liked to call out to her, but she was too far away. She would have liked to follow her, but somehow she daren't.

There went Lena in her blue dress, her best dress, right out there in the veld, where no white woman should ever walk alone, where she herself had never been alone, walking with a step not only jaunty and eager, but obviously purposeful. Why was Lena walking on and on, right out there, with that showy yellow scarf round her neck? All Maud's anger began to get up again, and her hand shook, so that the water which should have nourished a fern poured over on to the floor.

She was wondering what to do, when she saw young Jenson riding up, leading a horse with a saddle on its back. Good heavens, Lena must be going off, eloping, with that boy! Piet wouldn't get his grazing rights! Should she go and see if Lena had left a note on her dressing table?

The sky seemed strangely dark, the floor was unsteady under her feet. She sank into a chair and closed her eyes.

***

The next thing she knew was the voice of Annie, the maid. Maud opened her eyes, and started up quickly.

"Annie! What is it? What is the time? Why, it's nearly dark!"

"Please, missus, time for baby's bath."

They both hurried indoors, but Maud was the quickest.

In a few minutes she was stooping over the bath. The curtains were drawn, and the room was full of yellow lamplight. The baby sat up in the bath with a very straight back, and patted the surface of the water, which was in shadow, with its hands. Bright drops flickered in the light, and sprayed upwards on to Maud's face and neck. Her mouth protruded in an expression of strong, stupid yearning. All her thoughts and anxieties began to give way to pure feeling, and when she was drying the baby she pressed it against her, almost with violence.

"We don't care, do we, darling?" she said. "Who's mother's little own one and only? There, there, there, there, there."

When she got up, a brooch fell off her dress into the bath with a splash, and lay gleaming through the soapy water, where it seemed to be winking at her. She pressed her lips deep, deep with a furious kiss into the baby's soft white cheek. This sudden pressure made the infant's mouth project in an innocent pout, while its bright black eyes reflected tiny yellow dots of lamplight.

Intoxicated with joy, she closed her eyes and rocked herself from side to side, hugging the child, and oblivious, as she brushed with her lips the silk of its hair, of time and place, of her husband, her sister, and herself.

1927

Makapan's Caves

Herman Charles Bosman

Kaffirs?[18] (said Oom Schalk Lourens).[19] Yes, I know them. And they're all the same. I fear the Almighty, and I respect His works, but I could never understand why He made the kaffir and the rinderpest.[20] The Hottentot[21] is a little better. The Hottentot will only steal the biltong[22] hanging out on the line to dry. He won't steal the line as well. That is where the kaffir is different.

Still, sometimes you come across a good kaffir, who is faithful and upright and a true Christian and doesn't let the wild-dogs catch the sheep. I always think that it isn't right to kill that kind of kaffir.

I remember about one kaffir we had, by the name of Nongaas. How we got him was after this fashion. It was in the year of the big drought, when there was no grass, and the water in the pan had dried up. Our cattle died like flies. It was terrible. Every day ten or twelve or twenty died. So my father said we must pack everything on the wagons and trek up to the Dwarsberge, where he heard there had been good rains. I was six years old, then, the youngest in the family. Most of the time I sat in the back of the wagon, with my mother and my two sisters. My brother Hendrik was seventeen, and he helped my father and the kaffirs to drive on our cattle. That was how we trekked. Many more of our cattle died along the way, but after about

---

18 ... very offensive term for black South Africans

19 ... tory-telling character for whom Bosman's stories are famous

20 ... infectious cattle disease that broke out in South Africa in the late nineteenth century

21 ... very offensive term for the southern African Khoi people

22 ... dried meat (South African English)

two months we got into the Lowveld and my father said that God had been good to us. For the grass was green along the Dwarsberge.

One morning we came to some kaffir huts, where my father bartered two sacks of mealies[23] for a roll of tobacco. A piccanin[24] of about my own age was standing in front of a hut, and he looked at us all the time and grinned. But mostly he looked at my brother Hendrik. And that was not a wonder, either. Even in those days my brother Hendrik was careful about his appearance, and he always tried to be fashionably dressed. On Sundays he even wore socks. When we had loaded up the mealies, my father cut off a plug of Boertobacco and gave it to the piccanin, who grinned still more, so that we saw every one of his teeth, which were very white. He put the plug in his mouth and bit it. Then we all laughed. The piccanin looked just like a puppy that has swallowed a piece of meat, and turns his head sideways, to see how it tastes.

That was in the morning. We went right on until the afternoon, for my father wanted to reach Tweekoppiesfontein, where we were going to stand with our cattle for some time. It was late in the afternoon when we got there, and we started to outspan. Just as I was getting off the wagon, I looked round and saw something jumping quickly behind a bush. It looked like some animal, so I was afraid, and told my brother Hendrik, who took up his gun and walked slowly towards the bush. We saw, directly afterwards, that it was the piccanin whom we had seen that morning in front of the hut. He must have been following behind our wagons for about ten miles. He looked dirty and tired, but when my brother went up to him he began to grin again, and seemed very happy. We didn't know what to do with him, so Hendrik shouted to him to go home, and started throwing stones at him. But my father was a merciful man, and after he had heard Nongaas's story – for that was the name of the piccanin – he said he could stay with us, but he must be good, and not tell lies and steal, like the other kaffirs. Nongaas told us in the Sechuana

---

23 ... maize (South African English), also *mielie*

24 ... derogative term for a black child (not exclusively South African English)

language, which my father understood, that his father and mother had been killed by the lions, and that he was living with his uncle, whom he didn't like, but that he liked my brother Hendrik, and that was why he had followed our wagons.

Nongaas remained with us for many years. He grew up with us. He was a very good kaffir, and as time went by he became much attached to all of us. But he worshipped my brother Hendrik. As he grew older, my father sometimes spoke to Nongaas about his soul, and explained to him about God. But although he told my father that he understood, I could see that whenever Nongaas thought of God, he was really only thinking of Hendrik.

It was just after my twenty-first birthday that we got news that Hermanus Potgieter and his whole family had been killed by a kaffir tribe under Makapan. They also said that, after killing him, the kaffirs stripped off old Potgieter's skin and made wallets out of it in which to carry their dagga.[25] It was very wicked of the kaffirs to have done that, especially as dagga makes you mad and it is a sin to smoke it. A commando was called up from our district to go and attack the tribe and teach them to have respect for the white man's laws – and above all, to have more respect for the white man's skin. My mother and sisters baked a great deal of harde beskuit,[26] which we packed up, together with mealie-meal and biltong. We also took out the lead mould and melted bullets. The next morning my brother and I set out on horseback for Makapan's kraal.[27] We were accompanied by Nongaas, whom we took along with us to look after the horses and light the fires. My father stayed at home. He said that he was

---

25 ... a plant native to South Africa, smoking its dried leaves has effects similar to cannabis

26 ... rusk (Afrikaans)

27 ... village or cluster of huts in South Africa, may also refer to an enclosure for cattle and other farm animals (Afrikaans)

too old to go on commando, unless it was to fight the redcoats,[28] if there were still any left.

But he gave us some good advice.

"Don't forget to read your Bible, my sons," he called out as we rode away. "Pray the Lord to help you, and when you shoot always aim for the stomach." These remarks were typical of my father's deeply religious nature, and he also knew that it was easier to hit a man in the stomach than in the head: and it is just as good, because no man can live long after his intestines have been shot away.

Well, we rode on, my brother and I, with Nongaas following a few yards behind us on the pack-horse. Now and again we fell in with other burghers,[29] many of whom brought their wagons with them, until, on the third day, we reached Makapan's kraal, where the big commando had already gone into camp. We got there in the evening, and everywhere as far as we could see there were fires burning in a big circle. There were over two hundred wagons, and on their tents the fires shone red and yellow. We reported ourselves to the veldkornet,[30] who showed us a place where we could camp, next to the four Van Rensburg brothers. Nongaas had just made the fire and boiled the coffee when one of the Van Rensburgs came up and invited us over to their wagon. They had shot a rietbok[31] and were roasting pieces of it on the coals.

We all shook hands and said it was good weather for the mealies if only the ruspes[32] didn't eat them, and that it was time we had another president, and that rietbok tasted very fine when roasted on the coals. Then they told us what had happened about the kaffirs. Makapan and his followers had seen the commandos coming from

---

28 ... British troops, named after the red uniform they wore in the First Anglo-Boer War (1880-1881)

29 ... citizen (Afrikaans), descendants of the Dutch planters who had settled in the Cape Colony in the seventeenth century

30 ... local government official (Afrikaans)

31 ... reedbuck, small South African antelope (Afrikaans)

32 ... caterpillars (Afrikaans), also ruspers

a distance, and after firing a few shots at them had all fled into the caves in the krantz.[33] These caves stretched away underground very far and with many turnings. So, as the Boers could not storm the kaffirs without losing heavily, the kommandant[34] gave instructions that the ridge was to be surrounded and the kaffirs starved out. They were all inside the caves, the whole tribe, men, women and children. They had already been there six days, and as they couldn't have much food left, and as there was only a small dam with brackish water, we were hopeful of being able to kill off most of the kaffirs without wasting ammunition.

Already, when the wind blew towards us from the mouth of the caves, the stink was terrible. We would have pitched our camp further back, only that we were afraid some of the kaffirs would escape between the fires.

The following morning I saw for the first time why we couldn't drive the kaffirs from their lairs, even though our commando was four hundred strong. All over, through the rocks and bushes, I could see black openings in the krantz, that led right into the deep parts of the earth. Here and there we could see dead bodies lying. But there were still left a lot of kaffirs that were not dead and them we could not see. But they had guns, which they had bought from the illicit traders and the missionaries, and they shot at us whenever we came within range. And all the time there was that stench of decaying bodies.

For another week the siege went on. Then we heard that our leaders, Marthinus Wessels Pretorius and Paul Kruger, had quarrelled. Kruger wanted to attack the kaffirs immediately and finish the affair, but Pretorius said it was too dangerous and he didn't want any more burghers killed. He said that already the hand of the Lord lay heavy upon Makapan, and in another few weeks the kaffirs would all be dead of starvation. But Paul Kruger said that it would even be better if the hand of the Lord lay still heavier upon

---

33 ... steep cliff (South African English), also *krans* or *kranz*

34 ... commander (Afrikaans)

the kaffirs. Eventually Paul Kruger obtained permission to take fifty volunteers and storm the caves from one side, while Kommandant Piet Potgieter was to advance from the other side with two hundred men, to distract the attention of the kaffirs. Kruger was popular with all of us, and nearly everyone volunteered to go with him. So he picked fifty men, among whom were the Van Rensburgs and my brother. Therefore, as I did not want to stay behind and guard the camp, I had to join Piet Potgieter's commando.

All the preparations were made, and the following morning we got ready to attack. My brother Hendrik was very proud and happy at having been chosen for the more dangerous part. He oiled his gun very carefully and polished up his veldskoens.[35]

Then Nongaas came up and I noticed that he looked very miserable.

"My baas,"[36] he said to my brother Hendrik, "you mustn't go and fight. They'll shoot you dead."

My brother shook his head.

"Then let me go with you, baas," Nongaas said; "I will go in front and look after you."

Hendrik only laughed.

"Look here, Nongaas," he said, "you can stay behind and cook the dinner. I will get back in time to eat it."

The whole commando came together and we all knelt down and prayed. Then Marthinus Wessels Pretorius said we must sing Hymn Number 23, "Rest my soul, thy God is king." Furthermore, we sang another hymn and also a psalm. Most people would have thought that one hymn would be enough. But not so Pretorius. He always made quite sure of everything he did. Then we moved off to the attack. We fought bravely, but the kaffirs were many, and they lay in the darkness of the caves, and shot at us without our being able to see them. While the fighting lasted it was worse than the lyddite bombs

---

35 ... rough boots (Afrikaans), from *veld* "field" and *skoen* "shoe"

36 ...master, sir, employer, also used as a respectful address

at Paardeberg. And the stench was terrible. We tied handkerchiefs round the lower part of our face, but that did not help. Also, since we were not Englishmen, many of us had no handkerchiefs. Still we fought on, shooting at an enemy we could not see. We rushed right up to the mouth of one of the caves, and even got some distance into it, when our leader, Kommandant Piet Potgieter, flung up his hands and fell backwards, shot through the breast. We carried him out, but he was quite dead. So we lost heart and retired.

When we returned from the fight we found that the other attacking party had also been defeated. They had shot many kaffirs, but there were still hundreds of them left, who fought all the more fiercely with hunger gnawing at their bellies.

I went back to our camp. There was only Nongaas, sitting forward on a stone, with his face on his arms. An awful fear clutched me as I asked him what was wrong.

"Baas Hendrik," he replied, and as he looked at me in his eyes there was much sorrow, "Baas Hendrik did not come back."

I went out immediately and made enquiries, but nobody could tell me anything for sure. They remembered quite well seeing my brother Hendrik when they stormed the cave. He was right in amongst the foremost of the attackers. When I heard that, I felt a great pride in my brother, although I also knew that nothing else could be expected of the son of my father. But no man could tell me what had happened to him. All they knew was that when they got back he was not amongst them.

I spoke to Marthinus Wessels Pretorius and asked him to send out another party to seek for my brother. But Pretorius was angry.

"I will not allow one more man," he replied. "It was all Kruger's doing. I was against it from the start. Now Kommandant Potgieter has been killed, who was a better man than Kruger and all his Dopper clique put together. If any man goes back to the caves I shall discharge him from the commando."

But I don't think it was right of Pretorius. Because Paul Kruger was only trying to do his duty, and afterwards, when he was nominated for president, I voted for him.

It was eleven o'clock when I again reached our part of the laager.[37] Nongaas was still sitting on the flat stone, and I saw that he had carried out my brother Hendrik's instructions, and that the pot was boiling on the fire. The dinner was ready, but my brother was not there. That sight was too much for me, and I went and lay down alone under the Van Rensburgs' wagon.

I looked up again, about half an hour later, and I saw Nongaas walking away with a water-bottle and a small sack strapped to his back. He said nothing to me, but I knew he was going to look for my brother Hendrik. Nongaas knew that if his baas was still alive he would need him. So he went to him. That was all. For a long while I watched Nongaas as he crept along through the rocks and bushes. I supposed it was his intention to lie in wait near one of the caves and then crawl inside when the night came. That was a very brave thing to do. If Makapan's kaffirs saw him they would be sure to kill him, because he was helping the Boers against them, and also because he was a Bechuana.

The evening came, but neither my brother Hendrik nor Nongaas. All that night I sat with my face to the caves and never slept. Then in the morning I got up and loaded my gun. I said to myself that if Nongaas had been killed in the attempt there was only one thing left for me to do. I myself must go to my brother.

I walked out first into the veld, in case one of the officers saw me and made me come back. Then I walked along the ridge and got under cover of the bushes. From there I crawled along, hiding in the long grass and behind the stones, so that I came to one part of Makapan's stronghold where things were more quiet. I got to within about two hundred yards of a cave. There I lay very still, behind a big rock, to find out if there were any kaffirs watching from that side. Occasionally I heard the sound of a shot being fired, but that was far

---

37 … wagon fort for the protection of people and animals (Afrikaans)

away. Afterwards I fell asleep, for I was very weary with the anxiety and through not having slept the night before.

When I woke up the sun was right overhead. It was hot and there were no clouds in the sky. Only there were a few aasvoëls,[38] which flew round and round very slowly, without ever seeming to flap their wings. Now and again one of them would fly down and settle on the ground, and it was very horrible. I thought of my brother Hendrik and shivered. I looked towards the cave. Inside it seemed as though there was something moving. A minute later I saw that it was a kaffir coming stealthily towards the entrance. He appeared to be looking in my direction, and for fear that he should see me and call the other kaffirs, I jumped up quickly and shot at him, aiming at the stomach. He fell over like a sack of potatoes and I was thankful for my father's advice. But I had to act quickly. If the other kaffirs had heard the shot they would all come running up at once. And I didn't want that to happen. I didn't like the look of those aasvoëls. So I decided to take a great risk. Accordingly I ran as fast as I could towards the cave and rushed right into it, so that, even if the kaffirs did come, they wouldn't see me amongst the shadows. For a long time I lay down and waited. But as no more kaffirs came, I got up and walked slowly down a dark passage, looking round every time to see that nobody followed me, and to make sure that I would find my way back. For there were many twists and turnings, and the whole krantz seemed to be hollowed out.

I knew that my search would be very difficult. But there was something that seemed to tell me that my brother was nearby. So I was strong in my faith, and I knew that the Lord would lead me aright. And I found my brother Hendrik, and he was alive. It was with a feeling of great joy that I came across him. I saw him in the dim light that came through a big split in the roof. He was lying against a boulder, holding his leg and groaning. I saw afterwards that his leg was sprained and much swollen, but that was all that was wrong. So great was my brother Hendrik's surprise at seeing me

---

38 ... vulture (Afrikaans)

that at first he could not talk. He just held my hand and laughed softly, and when I touched his forehead I knew he was feverish. I gave him some brandy out of my flask, and in a few words he told me all that had happened. When they stormed the cave he was right in front and as the kaffirs retreated he followed them up. But they all ran in different ways, until my brother found himself alone. He tried to get back, but lost his way and fell down a dip. In that way he sprained his ankle so severely that he had been in agony all the time. He crawled into a far corner and remained there, with the danger and the darkness and his pain. But the worst of all was the stink of the rotting bodies.

"Then Nongaas came," my brother Hendrik said.

"Nongaas?" I asked him.

"Yes," he replied. "He found me and gave me food and water, and carried me on his back. Then the water gave out and I was very thirsty. So Nongaas took the bottle to go and fill it at the pan. But it is very dangerous to get there, and I am so frightened they may kill him."

"They will not kill him," I said. "Nongaas will come back." I said that, but in my heart I was afraid. For the caves were many and dark, and the kaffirs were blood-mad. It would not do to wait. So I lifted Hendrik on my shoulder and carried him towards the entrance. He was in much pain.

"You know," he whispered, "Nongaas was crying when he found me. He thought I was dead. He has been very good to me – so very good. Do you remember that day when he followed behind our wagons? He looked so very trustful and so little, and yet I – I threw stones at him. I wish I did not do that. I only hope that he comes back safe. He was crying and stroking my hair."

As I said, my brother Hendrik was feverish.

"Of course he will come back," I answered him. But this time I knew that I lied. For as I came through the mouth of the cave I kicked against the kaffir I had shot there. The body sagged over to one side and I saw the face.

1930

Mob Passion

D. Can Themba

There was a thick crowd on Platform Two, rushing for the 'All Stations' Randfontein train. Men, women and children were pushing madly to board the train. They were heaving and pressing, elbows in faces, bundles bursting, weak ones kneaded. Even at the opposite side people were balancing precariously to escape being shoved off the platform. Here and there deft fingers were exploring unwary pockets. Somewhere an outraged dignity was shrieking stridently, vilely cursing someone's parentage. The carriages became fuller and fuller. With a jerk the electric train moved out of the station.

"Whew!" sighed Lingo Sakwe. He gathered his few parcels upon his lap pressing his elbows to his side pockets. He did not really have any valuables in these pockets; only long habit was working instinctively now.

Linga was a tall, slender fellow, more man than boy. He was not particularly handsome; but he had those tense eyes of the young student who was ever inwardly protesting against some wrong or other. In fact at the moment he was not a student at all. He was working for a firm of lawyers in Market Street. He hoped to save enough money in a year or two to return to university to complete an arts degree which he had been forced by 'circumstances' to abandon.

People were still heaving about in the train but Linga was not annoyed. He knew that by the time the train reached Langlaagte, or Westbury, most of these folks would be gone and he would be able to breathe again. At Braamfontein many people alighted; but he was not thinking of his discomfort any more. He was thinking of Mapula now. She had promised that she would be in time for this train. That depended, of course, on whether she had succeeded in persuading the staff nurse in charge of the ward in which she worked to let her off early.

The train slowed down. Industria. Linga anxiously looked outside. Sure enough, there she was! He gave a wolf-whistle, as if he were admiring some girl he did not know. She hurried to his carriage, stepped in and sat beside him. They seemed not to know each other from Adam. An old man nearby was giving a lively account, in the grimmest terms, of the murders committed in Newclare.

At Westbury the atmosphere was tense. Everybody crowded at the windows to see. Everywhere there were white policemen, heavily armed. The situation was 'under control', but everyone knew that in the soul of almost every being in this area raved a seething madness, wild and passionate, with the causes lying deep. No cursory measures could remedy; no superficial explanation could illuminate. These jovial faces that could change into masks of bloodlust and destruction without warning, with the smallest provocation! There is a vicious technique faithfully applied in these riots. Each morning these people quietly rise, and with a business-like manner hurry to their work. Each evening they return to a Devil's Party, uncontrollably drawn into hideous orgies. Sometimes the violence would subside for weeks or months, and then suddenly would flare up at some unexpected spot, on some unexpected pretext.

At Newclare, too, from the train all seemed quiet. But Linga and Mapula knew the deceptive quiet meant the same even here. The train rushed on, emptier. Only when they had passed Maraisburg did these two venture to speak to each other. Linga was Xhosa and Mapula Sotho. A Letebele and a Russian! They had to be very careful! Love in its mysterious, often ill-starred ways had flung them together.

Linga spoke first.

"Sure you saw no one who might know you?" he asked softly.

"Eh-eh,"[39] she replied.

---

[39] ... from Ehe "yes" (isiZulu)

She fidgeted uneasily with the strap of her handbag. His hand went out and closed over her fingers. They turned simultaneously to look at each other.

A sympathetic understanding came into Linga's eyes. He smiled.

"Rather tense, isn't it?" he said.

She looked past him through the window.

"Witpoortjie!" she exclaimed. "Come, let's go."

She rose and went to the door. The train stopped and they went out. Together they walked to a bridge, went over the line and out by a little gate. For some two hundred yards they walked over flat, stubbly ground. Then they went down a mountain-cleft at the bottom of which ran a streamlet. They found a shady spot and sat down on the green grass. Then suddenly they fled into each other's arms like frightened children. The time-old ritual, ancient almost as the hills, always novel as the ever-changing skies. For a long time they clung to each other silently. Only the little stream gurgled its nonsense; these two daring hearts were lost to each other. The world, too – good, bad or indifferent – was forgotten in the glorious flux of their souls meeting and mingling.

At last Mapula spoke – half cried: "Oh, Linga! I'm afraid."

"*Here where the world is quiet?*" he quoted, with infinite softness. "No, dear, nothing can reach and harm us here." Then with a sigh: "Still, the cruellest thing they do is to drive two young people like guilty things to sneak off only to see each other. What is wrong with our people, Mapula?"

She did not answer. He lay musing for a long time. She could see that he was slowly getting angry. Sometimes she wished she could understand the strange indignations of his spirit and the great arguments by which he explained life. Most times she only yearned for his love.

"They do not see! They do not see!" he continued vehemently. "They butcher one another, and they seem to like it. Where there should be brotherhood and love, there are bitter animosities. Where there should be co-operation in common adversity, there are barriers of hostility, steeling a brother's heart against a brother's misery. Sometimes, 'Pule, I understand it. We have had so many dishonest leaders, and we have so often had our true leaders left in the lurch by weak-kneed colleagues and lukewarm followers, that no one wishes to stick his neck out too far. Where is the courage to weld these suicidal factions into a nation? The trouble is, very few of us have a vision comprehensive enough of our destiny! I believe *God has a few of us to whom He whispers in the ear*! Our true history is before us, for we yet have to build, to create, to achieve. Our very oppression is the flower of opportunity. If not for History's Grand Finale, why then does God hold us back? Hell! and here we are, feuding in God's dressing-room even before the curtain rises. Oh! –" He covered his face and fell into her lap, unable to say any more.

Instinctively Mapula fingered his hair. In God's dressing-room, she thought, What does it mean? But his anguish stabbed at her heart. Trying to forget herself she only sought within her a tenderness to quell the bitter wretchedness she had heard in his voice.

"Linga, no! Let me show you something else – something that I understand. It is not so long before you and I can marry, I dream about the home that we are going to have. I ... I want that home, Linga. You taught me that woman's greatest contribution to civilisation so far has been to furnish homes where great men and great ideas have developed. Moreover, there's our problem. Let us rather think of ways of handling my father. No, no; not now. Let us think about the present, about *now*."

Thabo was running faster now that he was nearing home. His mind was in a whirl; but he knew that he had to tell his father. The lop-sided gate was in the far corner, so he smartly leaped over the fence where it was slack. He stopped abruptly at the door. He always did when there were people. But now he soon realised these people were his two uncles – Uncle Alpheus and Uncle Frans. Somehow great news always brings a glory of prestige on the head of the bringer. Thabo felt himself almost a hero now; for these two men were die-hard stalwarts in the Russian cause. Uncle Alpheus was a romantic firebrand while Uncle Frans was a scheming character of the power-behind-the-throne variety. They were complementary to each other: together a formidable team.

"Father, where is he?" hissed Thabo, breathing hard. The excitement in his voice aroused everyone.

"Holy Shepherd! What's the matter, boy?" cried Uncle Alpheus.

"Mapula, Mapula. She loves with a Letebele."

"What!" exploded Uncle Alpheus. "Where is she?" Then more calmly: "Come'n, boy. Tell us everything more quietly; your father is out there?"

"J-J-Jonas t-t-tells me – J-Jonas is a boy who works with me – Jonas tells me that Mapula loves with a Letebele. They always meet at the hospital; but never in the sitting-room. He hopes to marry her."

"Never!" barked Alpheus. Just then the door burst open. A party of men carried in the limp form of Thabo's father. He was unconscious and blood streamed all over his face. Beyond them, just outside the door, a crowd had gathered. Everyone was at once asking what had happened. As the news spread, ugly moods swept the crowd. Ra-Thabo[40] was carried into the bedroom and tended by the women. Alpheus and Frans returned to the fore-room and conferred.

"What now?" Alpheus asked Frans.

"Of course, we must revenge. You will talk to the people – the women. Talk fire into them. Connect it with the Mapula business; that'll warm them. Suggest drugs – a Letebele must use drugs, mustn't he? I'll be in the house. Just when they begin to get excited I'll arrange to carry Ra-Thabo out – to the hospital, you know. See if we can't get them bad!" He smiled cheerlessly.

Outside, the crowd – mostly women – was thickening. Even in the streets they could be seen coming along in groups, blanketed men and women. From the house Thabo and his little sister, Martha,

---

40 ... Mr Thabo (isiZulu)

joined the crowd. It was obvious that their uncles were going to do something about it.

Alpheus stepped on to the little mud wall. He raised his left hand and the blanket over it rose with it. This movement was most dramatic. In a few moments the crowd moved closer to him and became silent. Then he began to speak. He began in a matter-of-fact voice, giving the bare fact that Ra-Thabo, their leader, had been hurt. Warming gradually he discussed the virtues of this man. Then he went on to tell of how this man had actually been hurt. Neither confused fighting nor cowardly brutalities rose in the mind as this man spoke, but a glorious picture of crusaders charging on in a holy cause behind their lion-hearted leader. Oh, what a clash there was! The Letebele were pushed beyond Westbury station. There the heroes met a rested, reinforced enemy. For a moment all that could be seen was the head of Ra-Thabo going down among them. The clang of battle could be heard; the furious charge could be seen, in the words of this man who was not there. The Basothos fought desperately and won so much ground that their all but lost leader could be rescued and carried back home. And what finds he there? Alpheus's voice went down softer and heavier, touching strings of pathos, rousing tragic emotions which the hearts present had never before experienced. There was an automatic movement in the crowd as everybody strained forward to hear. In awful, horror-filled whispers he told of Ra-Thabo's daughter giving herself to a Letebele. The thing is not possible! he hissed. It would not have happened if the maid had not been bewitched with drugs. Are they going to brook it! he cracked. No! all the throats roared. Are they ready for vengeance! Now! thundered the mob. Someone in the crowd shouted "*Mule!*"[41] Then the women took up their famous war-cry, chilling to a stranger, but driving the last doubting spirit there to frenzy and fury.

"*Ee!-le!-le!-le!-le!-le!-le!-Eu! Eu! Eu!*"[42]

---

41 … from *Mmulaye* "Kill him" (isiZulu)

42 … war cry, with exclamation marks to punctuate its rhythm (isiZulu)

Now they were prancing and swaying in uninterpretable rhythms. A possessed bard in their midst was chattering the praises of the dead, the living, and the unborn; his words clattering like the drumsticks of a fiend.

"Let us go past Maraisburg and attack them from the rear!" yelled Alpheus over the din.

At that moment the door of the house went open. The mob, which had been on the point of dashing out, recoiled. The sight they saw stunned them. Frans and two other men were carrying out Ra-Thabo, besmeared with blood. Thabo saw Uncle Alpheus leaping with trailing blanket and yelling "To Maraisburg!" Again he leaped over the fence into the street. The mob followed hard on his heels.

"*MULE!*" "*MULE!*" "*MULE!*"

As the last blanket swept round the corner, Frans turned back to the injured man. His two helpers had also been drawn in by the irresistible suction of the mob-feeling. With a smile he said to the unhearing Ra-Thabo: "I'll have to get a taxi to take you to hospital, brother." Then he carried him back into the house.

"All Change! All Change!" And more brusquely: "Come'n. *Puma! Puma!*"[43]

Linga and Mapula hurried out. News had arrived that trouble had started again at Newclare; more seriously than usual. All trains from Randfontein were being stopped here and sent back.

Shrugging, Linga drew Mapula away, and arm-in-arm they strolled along the platform, out by the little gate, into some suburban area. For a time they walked on in silence. Then Mapula spoke. "I hope I'll get back in time," she said.

"Then let's walk faster. We might get a lift outside the suburb." They walked into the open country. Linga knew that if he could only find a certain golf-course somewhere around here, he would know where the road was. Meanwhile, they had to stumble on over rough country, and Mapula's cork-heeled shoes were tormenting her toes.

---

43 ... from *Phuma* "Go out" (isiZulu)

She limped on as stoically as she could. Linga did not notice her suffering as he was looking out for familiar landmarks. Those trees looked suspiciously like the golf-course to him.

When they reached the trees Mapula said: "Linga, let us rest here; my toes are suffering."

"All right," he replied. "But I must look for the road. Let's look for a cool place where you may rest while I search for the golf-course."

"Mm."

He led her amongst the trees. She sat down and pulled off her shoes. When he thought he saw a shadow of distress flit across her brow he bent down, took her hand, pressed it and muttered: "Back in a moment, sweet." He rose slowly, looked at her indecisively, then turned away slowly and walked off.

He did not search far before he noticed a torn and faded flag. The hole was nearby. Suddenly he emerged from the cluster of trees, and came upon the road. But his attention was caught by a horde of Russians pursuing a woman who came flying towards Linga. This spelt trouble for the Letebele. But in a flash he thought of an idea. He spoke fluent Sesotho and believed he could pass for a Mosotho, possibly as a Russian. He quickly drew a white handkerchief from the pocket of his trousers, tied it round his head. This made him look like an active supporter of the Russian cause. Skirts flying, the woman sped past him. Facing the mob he shouted: "Helele!"[44]

All its wrath spent, the mob crowded round out of sheer curiosity. Some were even in a jocular mood now; one playing lustily on a concertina. But here and there Linga could see deadly weapons snatched up in their hasty exodus from Newclare. He spoke to them in fluent Sesotho, taking his idiom from Teyateyaneng. He asked if he was on the road to Newclare; he said that he worked in Roodepoort, but was going to Newclare because his uncle there wanted more man-power in the house. Won't they please tell him where this road was?

---

44 ... cry of joy (isiZulu)

"Che![45] It is no Letebele this; this is a child of our home," remarked Alpheus.

"Kgele![46] You speak it, man," said a burly fellow. Then everyone directed Linga to Newclare.

Just then Mapula came running, shoes in hand and stockings twisted round her neck.

"Linga! Linga, my darling! What are they doing to you!" she screamed as she forced her way through the crowd. Linga stiffened. When she reached him she flung her arm around him and clung to him with all her strength, crying all the time. Then she saw her uncle, stupefied like the rest of them, standing there. She ran to him and begged him to save her lover. He pushed her aside, walked up to Linga, and stood before him, arms akimbo.

"Ehe![47] So you are a Letebele after all. You lie so sleekly that I can understand why my daughter thinks she loves you." Then he swung round, his blanket trailing in an arc. "Friends, we need go no further. This is the dog that bewitched my brother's child. Let's waste no time with him. Tear him to pieces!" The mob rushed upon Linga: "*Mmate! Mmate!*"[48]

"Uncle! Uncle!" cried Mapula. But even as she cried she knew that nothing could be done. She had courted the contempt of her people; and she understood now that all her entreaties were falling upon deaf ears. Whether from convenience or superstition – it did not signify which – she was considered the victim of the Letebele's root-craft.

Suddenly from the scuffling mob flew an axe which fell at her feet. In a flash she knew her fate. Love, frustrated beyond bearing, bent her mind to the horrible deed.

---

45 ... no (Sesotho)

46 ... oh my God (Sesotho)

47 ... yes (isiZulu)

48 ... Hit/Beat him (isiZulu)

Mapula acted. Quickly she picked up the axe whilst the mob was withdrawing from its prey, several of them spattered with blood. With the axe in her hand Mapula pressed through them until she reached the inner, sparser group. She saw Alpheus spitting upon Linga's battered body. He turned with a guttural cackle – He-he-he! He-he-he! – into the descending axe. It sank into his neck and down he went. She stepped on his chest and pulled out the axe. The blood gushed out all over her face and clothes. With that evil-looking countenance she gradually turned to the stunned crowd, half lifting the axe and walking slowly but menacingly towards the largest group. They retreated – a hundred and twenty men and women retreated before this devil-possessed woman with the ghastly appearance. But then she saw the mangled body of the man she loved and her nerve snapped. The axe slipped from her hand and she dropped on Linga's body, crying piteously: "Jo-o! Jo-o! Jo-o! Jo-na-jo! Jo-na-jo!"

Someone came and lifted her up. Someone else was dragging Alpheus's bleeding corpse by the collar so that his shoes sprang out one after the other.

The crowd was going back now. All the bravado gone, they were quiet and sulky. Only the agonised wailing of Mapula could be heard. Every breast was quelled by a sense of something deeply wrong, a sense of outrage. The tumult in every heart, feeling individually now, was a human protest insistently seeking expression, and then that persistent wail of the anguished girl, torturing the innermost core of even the rudest conscience there. The men felt themselves before God; the women heard the denunciations of thwarted love. Within they were all crying bitterly: "Jo-o! Jo-o! Jo-nana-jo!"

1953

Sunlight in Trebizond Street

Alan Paton

Today the lieutenant said to me, *I'm going to do you a favour.* I don't answer him. I don't want his favours. *I'm not supposed to do it*, he said. *If I were caught I'd be in trouble.* He looks at me as though he wanted me to say something, and I could have said, *that'd break my heart,* but I don't say it. I don't speak unless I think it will pay me. That's my one fast rule.

Don't you want me to do you a favour? he asks. *I don't care*, I said, *if you do me a favour or you don't. But if you want to do it, that's your own affair.*

You're a stubborn devil, aren't you? I don't answer that, but I watch him. I have been watching Caspar for a long time, and I have come to the conclusion that he has a grudging respect for me. If the major knew his job, he'd take Caspar away, give me someone more exciting, more dangerous.

Don't you want to get out? I don't answer. There are two kinds of questions I don't answer, and he knows it. One is the kind he needs the answers to. The other is the kind to which he knows the answers already. Of course I want to get out, away from those hard staring eyes, whose look you can bear only if your own are hard and staring too. And I want to eat some tasty food, and drink some wine, in some place with soft music and hidden lights. And I want … but I do not think of that. I have made a rule.

How many days have you been here? I don't answer that, because I don't know any more. And I don't want Caspar to know that I don't. When they took away the first Bible, it was 81. By an effort of will that exhausted me, I counted up to 105. And I was right, up to 100 at any rate, for on that day they came to inform me, with almost a kind of ceremony, that duly empowered under Act so-and-so, Section so-and-so, they were going to keep me another 100, and would release me when I "answered satisfactorily". That shook me, though I tried to hide it from them. But I lost my head a little, and called out quite loudly, "Hooray for the rule of law." It was foolish. It achieved exactly nothing. After 105 I nearly went to pieces. The next morning I couldn't remember if it were 106 or 107. After that you can't remember any more. You lose your certitude. You're like a blind man who falls over a stool in the well-known house. There's no birthday, no trip to town, no letter from abroad, by which to remember. If you try going back, it's like going back to look for something you dropped yesterday in the desert, or in the forest, or in the water of the lake. Something is gone from you that you'll never find again.

It took me several days to convince myself that it didn't matter all that much. Only one thing mattered, and that was to give them no access to my private self. Our heroic model was B. B. B. He would not speak, or cry out, or stand up, or do anything they told him to do. He would not even look at them, if such a thing is possible. Solitude did not affect him, for he could withdraw into a solitude of his own, a kind of state of suspended being. He died in one such solitude. Some say he withdrew too far and could not come back. Others say he was tortured to death, that in the end the pain stabbed its way into the solitude. No one knows.

So far they haven't touched me. And if they touched me, what would I do? Pain might open the door to that private self. It's my fear of that that keeps me from being arrogant. I have a kind of superstition that pride gets punished sooner than anything else. It's a relic of my lost religion.

You're thinking deep, said Caspar, *I'll come tomorrow. I expect to bring you interesting news.*

***

Caspar said to me, *Rafael Swartz has been taken in.* It's all I can do to hide from him that for the first time I stand before him in my private and naked self. I dare not pull the clothes round me, for he would know what he had done. Why doesn't he bring instruments, to measure the sudden uncontrollable kick of the heart, and the sudden tensing of the muscles of the face, and the contraction of the pupils? Or does he think he can tell without them? He doesn't appear to be watching me closely. Perhaps he puts down the bait carelessly, confident that the prey will come. But does he not know that the prey is already a thousand times aware? I am still standing naked, but I try to look as though I am wearing clothes.

Rafael Swartz. Is he brave? Will he keep them waiting 1,000 days, till in anger they let him go? Or will he break as soon as one of them casually picks up the poker that has been left carelessly in the coals?

He's a rat, says Caspar. *He has already ratted on you.* I say foolishly, *How can he rat on me? I'm here already.*

You're here, Caspar agreed. He said complainingly, *But you don't tell us anything. Swartz is going to tell us things that you won't tell. Things you don't want us to know. Tell me, doctor, who's the boss?*

I don't answer him. I begin to feel my clothes stealing back on me. I could now look at Caspar confidently, but that I mustn't do. I must wait till I can do it casually.

I don't know when I'll see you again, he said, quite like conversation. *I'll be spending time with Swartz. I expect to have interesting talks with him. And if there's anything I think you ought to know, I'll be right back. Goodbye, doctor.*

He stops at the door. *There's one thing you might like to know. Swartz thinks you brought him in.*

He looks at me. *He thinks that,* he says, *because we told him so.*

***

John Forrester always said to me when parting, *Have courage.* Have I any courage? Have I any more courage than Rafael Swartz? And who am I to know the extent of his courage? Perhaps they are lying to me. Perhaps when they told him I had brought him in, he laughed at them and said, *It's an old trick but you can't catch an old dog with it.*

Don't believe them, Rafael. And I shan't believe them either. Have courage, Rafael, and I shall have courage too.

***

Caspar doesn't come. It's five days now. At least I think it's five. I can't even be sure of that now. Have courage, Rafael.

***

It must be ten days now. I am not myself. My stomach is upset. I go to and fro the whole day, and it leaves me weak and drained. But though my body is listless, my imagination works incessantly. What is happening there, in some other room, like this, perhaps in this building too? I know it is useless imagining it, but I go on with it. I've stopped saying, *Have courage, Rafael*, on the grounds that if he has lost his courage, it's too late, and if he hasn't lost his courage, it's superfluous. But I'm afraid. It's coming too close.

***

Who's your boss? asks Caspar, and of course I don't reply. He talks about Rafael Swartz and Lofty Coombe and Helen Columbus, desultory talk, with now and then desultory questions. The talk and the questions are quite pointless. Is the lieutenant a fool or is he not?

He says to me, *You're a dark horse, aren't you, doctor? Leading a double life, and we didn't know.*

I am full of fear. It's coming too close. I can see John Forrester now, white-haired and benevolent, what they call a man of distinction, the most miraculous blend of tenderness and steel that any of us will ever know. He smiles at me as though to say, *Keep up your courage, we're thinking of you every minute of the day.*

What does Caspar mean, my double life? Of course I led a double life, that's why I'm here. Does he mean some other double life? And how would they know? Could Rafael have known?

Can't you get away, my love? I'm afraid of you, I'm afraid for us all. What did I tell you? I can't remember. I swore an oath to tell no one. But with you I can't remember. And I swore an oath that there would never be any woman at all. That was my crime.

When I first came here, I allowed myself to remember you once a day, for about one minute. But now I am thinking of you more and more. Not just love, fear too. Did I tell you who we were?

Love, why don't you go? Tell them you didn't know I was a revolutionary. Tell them anything, but go.

As for myself, my opinion of myself is unspeakable. I thought I was superior, that I could love a woman, and still be remote and unknowable. We take up this work like children. We plot and plan and are full of secrets. Everything is secret except our secrecy.

***

What is happening now? Today the major comes with the lieutenant, and the mere sight of him sets my heart pounding. The major's not like Caspar. He does not treat me as superior or inferior. He says, *Sit down*, and I sit. He says to me, *So you still won't cooperate?* Such is my foolish state that I say to him, *Why should I cooperate? There's no law which says I must cooperate. In fact the law allows for my not cooperating, and gives you the power to detain me until I do.*

The major speaks to me quite evenly. He says, *Yes, I can detain you, but I can do more than that, I can break you. I can send you out of here an old broken man, going about with your head down, mumbling to yourself, like Samuelson.*

He talks to me as though I were an old man already. *You wouldn't like that, doctor. You like being looked up to by others. You like to pity others, it gives you a boost, but it would be hell to be pitied by them. In Fordsville they thought the sun shone out your eyes. Our name stinks down there because we took you away.*

We can break you, doctor, he said. *We don't need to give you shock treatment, or hang you up by the feet, or put a vice on your testicles. There are many other ways. But it isn't convenient. We don't want you drooling round Fordsville.* He adds sardonically, *It would spoil our image.*

He looks at me judicially, but there's a hard note in his voice. *It's inconvenient, but there may be no other way. And if there's no other way, we'll break you. Now listen carefully. I'm going to ask you a question.*

He keeps quiet for a minute, perhaps longer. He wants me to think over his threat earnestly. He says, *Who's your boss?*

After five minutes he stands up. He turns to Caspar. *All right, lieutenant, you can go ahead.*

***

What can Caspar go ahead with? Torture? for me? or for Rafael Swartz? My mind shies away from the possibility that it might be for you. But what did he mean by the double life? Their cleverness, which might some other time have filled me with admiration, fills me now with despair. They drop a fear into your mind, and then they go away. They're busy with other things, intent on their job of breaking, but you sit alone for days and think about the last thing they said. Ah, I am filled with fear for you. There are 3,000 million people in the world, and I can't get one of them to go to you and say, *Get out, this day, this very minute.*

***

Barbara Trevelyan, says Caspar, *it's a smart name. You covered it up well, doctor, so we're angry at you. But there's someone angrier than us. Didn't you promise on oath to have no friendship outside the People's League, more especially with a woman? What is your boss going to say?*

Yes, I promised. But I couldn't go on living like that, cut off from all love, from all persons, from all endearment. I wanted to mean something to somebody, a live person, not a cause. I am filled with shame, not so much that I broke my promise, but because I couldn't make an island where there was only our love, only you and me. But the world had to come in, and the great plan for the transformation of the world, and forbidden knowledge, dangerous knowledge, and … I don't like to say it, perhaps boasting came in too, dangerous boasting. My head aches with pain, and I try to remember what I told you.

You are having your last chance today, says Caspar. *If you don't talk today, you won't need to talk any more. Take your choice. Do you want her to tell us, or will you?*

I don't know. If I talk, then what was the use of these 100 days? Some will go to prison, some may die. If I don't tell, if I let her tell, then they will suffer just the same. And the shame will be just as terrible.

It doesn't matter, says Caspar, *if you tell or she tells. They'll kill you either way. Because we're going to let you go.*

He launches another bolt at me. *You see, doctor, she doesn't believe in the cause, she believes only in you. Tomorrow she won't even do that. Because we're going to tell her that you brought her in.*

Now he is watching me closely. Something is moving on my face. Is it an insect? Or a drop of sweat? Don't tell them, my love. Listen my love, I am sending a message to you. Don't tell them, my love.

Do you remember what Rafael Swartz used to boast at those meetings in the good old days, that he'd follow you to hell? Well, he'd better start soon, hadn't he? Because that's where you are now.

He takes off his watch and puts it on the table. *I give you five minutes*, he said, *and they're the last you'll ever get. Who's your boss?* He puts his hands on the table too, and rests his forehead on them. Tired he is, tired with breaking men. He lifts his head and puts on his watch and stands up. There is a look on his face I haven't seen before, hating and vicious.

You're all the same, aren't you? Subversion most of the time, and women in between. Marriage, children, family, that's for the birds, that's for our decadent society. You want to be free, don't you? You paint FREEDOM all over the damn town. Well you'll be free soon, and it'll be the end of you.

***

Lofty and Helen and Le Grange. And now Rafael. Is there anyone they can't break? Does one grow stronger or weaker as the days go by? I say a prayer for you tonight, to whatever God may be …

Did I say Rafael's name? I'm sorry, Rafael, I'm not myself today. Have courage, Rafael. Don't believe what they say. And I shan't believe either.

***

5 days? 7 days? More? I can't remember. I hardly sleep now. I think of you and wonder what they are doing to you. I try to remember what I told you. Did I tell you I was deep in? Did I tell you how deep? Did I tell you any of their names? It's a useless question, because I don't know the answer to it. If the answer came suddenly into my mind, I wouldn't know it for what it was.

Ah, never believe that I brought you in. It's an old trick, the cruellest trick of the cruellest profession in the world. Have courage, my love. Look at them out of your grey honest eyes and tell them you don't know anything at all, that you were just a woman in love.

***

Caspar says to me, *You're free.* What am I supposed to do? Should my face light up with joy? It might have done, only a few days ago. *Do you know why we're letting you go?* Is there point in not answering? I shake my head.

Because we've found your boss, that's why. When he sees I am wary, not knowing whether to believe or disbelieve, he says, *John Forrester's the name. He doesn't know what to believe either, especially when we told him you had brought him in. Doctor, don't come back here any more. You're not made for this game. You've only lasted this long because of orders received. Don't ask me why. Come, I'll take you home.*

***

Outside in the crowded street the sun is shining. The sunlight falls on the sooty trees in Trebizond Street, and the black leaves dance in the breeze. The city is full of noise and life, and laughter too, as though no one cared what might go on behind those barricaded walls. There is an illusion of freedom in the air.

1966

Death of a Son

Njabulo S. Ndebele

At last we got the body. Wednesday. Just enough time for a Saturday funeral. We were exhausted. Empty. The funeral still ahead of us. We had to find the strength to grieve. There had been no time for grief, really. Only much bewilderment and confusion. Now grief. For isn't grief the awareness of loss?

That is why when we finally got the body, Buntu said: "Do you realise our son is dead?" I realised. Our awareness of the death of our first and only child had been displaced completely by the effort to get his body. Even the horrible events that caused the death: we did not think of them, as such. Instead, the numbing drift of things took over our minds: the pleas, letters to be written, telephone calls to be made, telegrams to be dispatched, lawyers to consult, 'influential' people to 'get in touch with', undertakers to be contacted, so much walking and driving. That is what suddenly mattered: the irksome details that blur the goal (no matter how terrible it is), each detail becoming a door which, once unlocked, revealed yet another door. Without being aware of it, we were distracted by the smell of the skunk and not by what the skunk had done.

We realised something too, Buntu and I, that during the two-week effort to get our son's body, we had drifted apart. For the first time in our marriage, our presence to each other had become a matter of habit. He was there. He'll be there. And I'll be there. But when Buntu said: "Do you realise our son is dead?" he uttered a thought that suddenly brought us together again. It was as if the return of the body of our son was also our coming together. For it was only at that moment that we really began to grieve; as if our lungs had suddenly begun to take in air when just before, we were beginning to suffocate. Something with meaning began to emerge.

We realised. We realised that something else had been happening to us, adding to the terrible events. Yes, we had drifted apart. Yet, our estrangement, just at that moment when we should have been together, seemed disturbingly comforting to me. I was comforted in a manner I did not quite understand.

The problem was that I had known all along that we would have to buy the body anyway. I had known all along. Things would end that way. And when things turned out that way, Buntu could not look me in the eye. For he had said: "Over my dead body! Over my dead body!" as soon as we knew we would be required to pay the police or the government for the release of the body of our child.

"Over my dead body! Over my dead body!" Buntu kept on saying.

Finally, we bought the body. We have the receipt. The police insisted we take it. That way, they would be 'protected'. It's the law, they said.

I suppose we could have got the body earlier. At first I was confused, for one is supposed to take comfort in the heroism of one's man. Yet, inwardly, I could draw no comfort from his outburst. It seemed hasty. What sense was there to it when all I wanted was the body of my child? What would happen if, as events unfolded, it became clear that Buntu would not give up his life? What would happen? What would happen to him? To me?

For the greater part of two weeks, all of Buntu's efforts, together with friends, relatives, lawyers and the newspapers, were to secure release of the child's body without the humiliation of having to pay for it. A 'fundamental principle'.

Why was it difficult for me to see the wisdom of the principle? The worst thing, I suppose, was worrying about what the police may have been doing to the body of my child. How they may have been busy prying it open 'to determine the cause of death'?

Would I want to look at the body when we finally got it? To see further mutilations in addition to the 'cause of death'? What kind of mother would not want to look at the body of her child? people will ask. Some will say: "It's grief." She is too grief-stricken.

"But still ... ," they will say. And the elderly among them may say: "Young people are strange."

But how can they know? It was not that I would not want to see the body of my child, but that I was too afraid to confront the horrors of my own imagination. I was haunted by the thought of how useless it had been to have created something. What had been the point of it all? This body filling up with a child. The child steadily growing into something that could be seen and felt. Moving, as it always did, at that time of day when I was all alone at home waiting for it. What had been the point of it all?

How can they know that the mutilation to determine 'the cause of death' ripped my own body? Can they think of a womb feeling hunted? Disgorged?

And the milk that I still carried. What about it? What had been the point of it all?

Even Buntu did not seem to sense that that principle, the 'fundamental principle', was something too intangible for me at that moment, something that I desperately wanted should assume the form of my child's body. He still seemed far from ever knowing.

I remember one Saturday morning early in our courtship, as Buntu and I walked hand-in-hand through town, window-shopping. We cannot even be said to have been window-shopping, for we were aware of very little that was not ourselves. Everything in those windows was merely an excuse for words to pass between us.

We came across three girls sitting on the pavement, sharing a packet of fish and chips after they had just bought it from a nearby Portuguese cafe. Buntu said: "I want fish and chips too." I said: "So seeing is desire." I said: "My man is greedy!" We laughed. I still remember how he tightened his grip on my hand. The strength of it!

Just then, two white boys coming in the opposite direction suddenly rushed at the girls, and, without warning, one of them kicked the packet of fish and chips out of the hands of the girl who was holding it. The second boy kicked away the rest of what remained in the packet. The girl stood up, shaking her hand as if to throw off the pain in it. Then she pressed it under her armpit as if to squeeze the pain out of it. Meanwhile, the two boys went on their way laughing. The fish and chips lay scattered on the pavement and on the street like stranded boats on a river that had gone dry.

"Just let them do that to you!" said Buntu, tightening once more his grip on my hand as we passed on like sheep that had seen many of their own in the flock picked out for slaughter. We would note the event and wait for our turn. I remember I looked at Buntu, and saw his face was somewhat glum. There seemed no connection between that face and the words of reassurance just uttered. For a while, we went on quietly. It was then that I noticed his grip had grown somewhat limp. Somewhat reluctant. Having lost its self-assurance, it seemed to have been holding on because it had to, not because of a confident sense of possession.

It was not to be long before his words were tested. How could fate work this way, giving to words meanings and intentions they did not carry when they were uttered? I saw that day, how the language of love could so easily be trampled underfoot, or scattered like fish and chips on the pavement, and left stranded and abandoned like boats in river that suddenly went dry. Never again was love to be confirmed with words. The world around us was too hostile for vows of love. At any moment, the vows could be subjected to the stress of proof. And love died. For words of love need not be tested.

On that day, Buntu and I began our silence. We talked and laughed, of course, but we stopped short of words that would demand proof of action. Buntu knew. He knew the vulnerability of words. And so he sought to obliterate words with acts that seemed to promise redemption.

On that day, as we continued with our walk in town, that Saturday morning, coming up towards us from the opposite direction, was a burly Boer walking with his wife and two children. They approached Buntu and me with an ominously determined advance. Buntu attempted to pull me out of the way, but I never had a chance. The Boer shoved me out of the way, as if clearing a path for his family. I remember, I almost crashed into a nearby fashion display window. I remember, I glanced at the family walking away, the mother and the father each dragging a child. It was for one of those children that I had been cleared away. I remember, also, that as my tears came out, blurring the Boer family and everything else, I saw and felt deeply what was inside of me: a desire to be avenged.

But nothing happened. All I heard was Buntu say: "The dog!" At that very moment, I felt my own hurt vanish like a wisp of smoke. And as my hurt vanished, it was replaced, instead, by a tormenting desire to sacrifice myself for Buntu. Was it something about the powerlessness of the curse and the desperation with which it had been made? The filling of stunned silence with an utterance? Surely it ate into him, revealing how incapable he was of meeting the call of his words.

And so it was, that that afternoon, back in the township, left to ourselves at Buntu's home, I gave in to him for the first time. Or should I say I offered myself to him? Perhaps from some vague sense of wanting to heal something in him? Anyway, we were never to talk about that event. Never. We buried it alive deep inside of me that afternoon. Would it ever be exhumed? All I vaguely felt and knew was that I had the keys to the vault. That was three years ago, a year before we married.

The cause of death? One evening I returned home from work, particularly tired after I had been covering more shootings by the police in the East Rand. Then I had hurried back to the office in Johannesburg to piece together on my typewriter the violent scenes of the day, and then to file my report to meet the deadline. It was late when I returned home, and when I got there, I found a crowd of people in the yard. They were those who could not get inside. I panicked. What had happened? I did not ask those who were outside, being desperate to get into the house. They gave way easily when they recognised me.

Then I heard my mother's voice. Her cry rose well above the noise. It turned into a scream when she saw me. "What is it, mother?" I asked, embracing her out of a vaguely despairing sense of terror. But she pushed me away with an hysterical violence that astounded me.

"What misery have I brought you, my child?" she cried. At that point many women in the room began to cry too. Soon, there was much wailing in the room, and then all over the house. The sound of it! The anguish! Understanding, yet eager for knowledge, I became desperate. I had to hold onto something. The desire to embrace my mother no longer had anything to do with comforting her; for whatever she had done, whatever its magnitude, had become inconsequential. I needed to embrace her for all the anguish that tied everyone in the house into a knot. I wanted to be part of that knot, yet I wanted to know what had brought it about.

Eventually, we found each other, my mother and I, and clasped each other tightly. When I finally released her, I looked around at the neighbours and suddenly had a vision of how that anguish had to be turned into a simmering kind of indignation. The kind of indignation that had to be kept at bay only because there was a higher purpose at that moment: the sharing of concern.

Slowly and with a calmness that surprised me, I began to gather the details of what had happened. Instinctively, I seemed to have been gathering notes for a news report.

It happened during the day, when the soldiers and the police that had been patrolling the township in their Casspirs[49] began to shoot in the streets at random. Need I describe what I did not see? How did the child come to die just at that moment when the police and the soldiers began to shoot at random, at any house, at any mov-

---

49 ... a mine-proof military vehicle used by the South African police during apartheid to control and exercise power over township communities

ing thing? That was how one of our windows was shattered by a bullet. And that was when my mother, who looked after her grandchild when we were away at work, panicked. She picked up the child and ran to the neighbours. It was only when she entered the neighbour's house that she noticed the wetness of the blanket that covered the child she held to her chest as she ran for the sanctuary of neighbours. She had looked at her unaccountably bloody hand, then she noted the still bundle in her arms, and began at that moment to blame herself for the death of her grandchild ...

Later, the police, on yet another round of shooting, found people gathered at our house. They stormed in, saw what had happened. At first, they dragged my mother out, threatening to take her away unless she agreed not to say what had happened. But then they returned and, instead, took the body of the child away. By what freak of logic did they hope that by this act their carnage would never be discovered?

That evening, I looked at Buntu closely. He appeared suddenly to have grown older. We stood alone in an embrace in our bedroom. I noticed, when I kissed his face, how his once lean face had grown suddenly puffy.

At that moment, I felt the familiar impulse come upon me once more, the impulse I always felt when I sensed that Buntu was in some kind of danger, the impulse to yield something of myself to him. He wore the look of someone struggling to gain control of something. Yet, it was clear he was far from controlling anything. I knew that look. Had seen it many times. It came at those times when I sensed that he faced a wave that was infinitely stronger than he, that it would certainly sweep him away, but that he had to seem to be struggling. I pressed myself tightly to him as if to vanish into him; as if only the two of us could stand up to the wave.

"Don't worry," he said. "Don't worry. I'll do everything in my power to right this wrong. Everything. Even if it means suing the police!" We went silent.

I knew that silence. But I knew something else at that moment: that I had to find a way of disengaging myself from the embrace.

Suing the police? I listened to Buntu outlining his plans. "Legal counsel. That's what we need," he said. "I know some people in Pretoria," he said. As he spoke, I felt the warmth of intimacy between us cooling. When he finished, it was cold. I disengaged from his embrace slowly, yet purposefully. Why had Buntu spoken?

Later, he was to speak again, when all his plans had failed to work: "Over my dead body! Over my dead body!"

He sealed my lips. I would wait for him to feel and yield one day to all the realities of misfortune.

Ours was a home, it could be said. It seemed a perfect life for a young couple: I, a reporter; Buntu, a personnel officer at an American factory manufacturing farming implements. He had travelled to the United States and returned with a mind fired with dreams. We dreamed together. Much time we spent, Buntu and I, trying to make a perfect home. The occasions are numerous on which we paged through *Femina*, *Fair Lady*, *Cosmopolitan*, *Home Garden*, *Car*, as if somehow we were going to surround our lives with the glossiness in the magazines. Indeed, much of our time was spent window-shopping through the magazines. This time, it was different from the window-shopping we did that Saturday when we courted. This time our minds were consumed by the things we saw and dreamed of owning: the furniture, the fridge, TV, videocassette recorders, washing machines, even a vacuum cleaner and every other imaginable thing that would ensure a comfortable modern life.

Especially when I was pregnant. What is it that Buntu did not buy, then? And when the boy was born, Buntu changed the car. A family, he would say, must travel comfortably.

The boy became the centre of Buntu's life. Even before he was born, Buntu had already started making inquiries at white private schools. That was where he would send his son, the bearer of his name.

Dreams! It is amazing how the horrible findings of my newspaper reports often vanished before the glossy magazines of our dreams, how I easily forgot that the glossy images were concocted out of the keys of typewriters, made by writers whose business was to sell dreams at the very moment that death pervaded the land. So powerful are words and pictures that even their makers often believe in them.

Buntu's ordeal was long. So it seemed. He would get up early every morning to follow up the previous day's leads regarding the body of our son. I wanted to go with him, but each time I prepared to go he would shake his head.

"It's my task," he would say. But every evening he returned, empty-handed, while with each day that passed and we did not know where the body of my child was, I grew restive and hostile in a manner that gave me much pain. Yet Buntu always felt compelled to give a report on each day's events. I never asked for it. I suppose it was his way of dealing with my silence.

One day he would say: "The lawyers have issued a court order that the body be produced. The writ of *habeas corpus.*"[50]

On another day he would say: "We have petitioned the Minister of Justice."

On yet another he would say: "I was supposed to meet the Chief Security Officer. Waited the whole day. At the end of the day they said I would see him tomorrow if he was not going to be too busy. They are stalling."

Then he would say: "The newspapers, especially yours, are raising the hue and cry. The government is bound to be embarrassed. It's a matter of time."

And so it went on. Every morning he got up and left. Sometimes alone, sometimes with friends. He always left to bear the failure alone.

---

50 ... court order according to which a person under arrest has to be brought before a court or judge

How much did I care about lawyers, petitions and Chief Security Officers? A lot. The problem was that whenever Buntu spoke about his efforts, I heard only his words. I felt in him the disguised hesitancy of someone who wanted reassurance without asking for it. I saw someone who got up every morning and left not to look for results, but to search for something he could only have found with me.

And each time he returned, I gave my speech to my eyes. And he answered without my having parted my lips. As a result, I sensed, for the first time in my life, a terrible power in me that could make him do anything. And he would never ever be able to deal with that power as long as he did not silence my eyes and call for my voice.

And so, he had to prove himself. And while he left each morning, I learned to be brutally silent. Could he prove himself without me? Could he? Then I got to know, those days, what I'd always wanted from him. I got to know why I have always drawn him into me whenever I sensed his vulnerability.

I wanted him to be free to fear. Wasn't there greater strength that way? Had he ever lived with his own feelings? And the stress of life in this land: didn't it call out for men to be heroes? And should they live up to it even though the details of the war to be fought may often be blurred? They should.

Yet it is precisely for that reason that I often found Buntu's thoughts lacking in strength. They lacked the experience of strife that could only come from a humbling acceptance of fear and then, only then, the need to fight it.

Me? In a way, I have always been free to fear. The prerogative of being a girl. It was always expected of me to scream when a spider crawled across the ceiling. It was known I would jump onto a chair whenever a mouse blundered into the room.

Then, once more, the Casspirs came. A few days before we got the body back, I was at home with my mother when we heard the great roar of truck engines. There was much running and shouting in the streets. I saw them, as I've always seen them on my assignments: the Casspirs. On five occasions they ran down our street at great speed, hurling tear-gas canisters at random. On the fourth occasion, they got our house. The canister shattered another window and filled the house with the terrible pungent choking smoke that I had got to know so well. We ran out of the house gasping for fresh air.

So, this was how my child was killed? Could they have been the same soldiers? Now hardened to their tasks? Or were they new ones being hardened to their tasks? Did they drive away laughing? Clearing paths for their families? What paths?

And was this our home? It couldn't be. It had to be a little bird's nest waiting to be plundered by a predator bird. There seemed no sense to the wedding pictures on the walls, the graduation pictures, birthday pictures, pictures of relatives, and paintings of lush landscapes. There seemed no sense anymore to what seemed recognisably human in our house. It took only a random swoop to obliterate personal worth, to blot out any value there may have been to the past. In desperation, we began to live only for the moment. I do feel hunted.

It was on the night of the tear gas that Buntu came home, saw what had happened, and broke down in tears. They had long been in the coming…

My own tears welled out too. How much did we have to cry to refloat stranded boats? I was sure they would float again.

A few nights later, on the night of the funeral, exhausted, I lay on my bed, listening to the last of the mourners leaving. Slowly, I became conscious of returning to the world. Something came back after it seemed not to have been there for ages. It came as a surprise, as a reminder that we will always live around what will happen. The sun will rise and set, and the ants will do their endless work, until one day the clouds turn grey and rain falls, and even in the township, the ants will fly out into the sky. Come what may.

My moon came, in a heavy surge of blood. And, after such a long time, I remembered the thing Buntu and I had buried in me. I felt it as if it had just entered. I felt it again as it floated away on the surge. I would be ready for another month. Ready as always, each and every month, for new beginnings.

And Buntu? I'll be with him, now. Always. Without our knowing, all the trying events had prepared for us new beginnings. Shall we not prevail?

1987

Look-Alikes

Nadine Gordimer

It was scarcely worth noticing at first; an out-of-work lying under one of the rare indigenous shrubs cultivated by the Botany Department on campus. Some of us remembered, afterwards, having passed him. And he – or another like him – was seen rummaging in the refuse bins behind the Student Union; one of us (a girl, of course) thrust out awkwardly to him a pitta she'd just bought for herself at the canteen, and she flushed with humiliation as he turned away mumbling. When there were more of them, the woman in charge of catering came out with a kitchen-hand in a blood-streaked apron to chase them off like a band of marauding monkeys.

We were accustomed to seeing them pan-handling in the streets of the city near the university and gathered in this vacant lot or that, clandestine with only one secret mission, to beg enough to buy another bottle; moving on as the druids' circle of their boxes and bits of board spread on the ground round the ashes of their trash fires was cleared for the erection of postmodern office blocks. We all knew the one who waved cars into empty parking bays. We'd all been confronted, as we crossed the road or waited at the traffic lights, idling in our minds as the engine of the jalopy idles, by the one who held up a piece of cardboard with a message running out of space at the edges: NO JOB IM HUNGRY EVEYONE HELP PLeas.

At first; yes, there were already a few of them about. They must have drifted in by the old, unfrequented entrance down near the tennis courts, where the security fence was not yet completed. And if they were not come upon, there were the signs: trampled spaces in the bushes, empty bottles, a single split shoe with a sole like a lolling tongue. No doubt they had been chased out by a patrolling security guard. No student, at that stage, would have bothered to report the harmless presence; those of us who had cars might have been more careful than usual to leave no sweaters or radios visible through the locked windows. We followed our familiar rabbit-runs from the lecture rooms and laboratories back, forth and around campus, between residences, libraries, Student Union and swimming pool, through avenues of posters making announcements of debates and sports events, discos and rap sessions, the meetings of Muslim, Christian or Jewish brotherhoods, gay or feminist sisterhoods, with the same lack of attention to all but the ones we'd put up ourselves.

It was summer when it all started. We spend a lot of time on the lawns around the pool, in summer. We swot down there, we get a good preview of each other more or less nude, boys and girls, there's plenty of what you might call foreplay – happy necking. And the water to cool off in. The serious competitive swimmers come early in the morning when nobody else is up, and it was they who discovered these people washing clothes in the pool. When the swimmers warned them off they laughed and jeered. One left a dirt-stiff pair of pants that a swimmer balled and threw after him. There was argument among the swimmers; one felt the incident ought to be reported to Security, two were uncomfortable with the idea in view of the university's commitment to being available to the city community. They must have persuaded him that he would be exposed for elitism, because although the pool was referred to as The Wishee-Washee, among us, after that, there seemed to be no action taken.

Now you began to see them all over. Some greeted you smarmily (*my baas*,[51] sir, according to their colour and culture), retreating humbly into the undergrowth, others, bold on wine or stoned on meths, sentimental on pot, or transformed in the wild hubris of all three, called out a claim (Hey man, *Ja boetie*)[52] and even beckoned to you to join them where they had formed one of their circles, or huddled, just two, with the instinct for seclusion that only couples

---

51 ... master, sir, employer, also used as a respectful address

52 ... yes brother (Afrikaans)

looking for a place to make love have, among us. The security fence down at the tennis courts was completed, reinforced with spikes and manned guard-house, but somehow they got in. The guards with their Alsatian dogs patrolled the campus at night but every day there were more shambling figures disappearing into the trees, more of those thick and battered faces looking up from the wells between buildings, more supine bodies contoured like sacks of grass-cuttings against the earth beneath the struts of the sports grandstands.

And they were no longer a silent presence. Their laughter and their quarrels broadcast over our student discussions, our tête-à-tête conversations and love-making, even our raucous fooling about. They had made a kind of encampment for themselves, there behind the sports fields where there was a stretch of ground whose use the university had not yet determined: it was for future expansion of some kind, and in the meantime equipment for maintenance of the campus was kept there — objects that might or might not be useful, an old tractor, barrels for indoor plants when the Vice-Chancellor requested a bower to decorate some hall for the reception of distinguished guests, and — of course — the compost heaps. The compost heaps were now being used as a repository for more than garden waste. If they had not been there with their odours of rot sharpened by the chemical agents for decay with which they were treated, the conclave living down there might have been sniffed out sooner. Perhaps they had calculated this in the secrets of living rough: perhaps they decided that the Alsatians' noses would be bamboozled.

So we knew about them — everybody knew about them, students, faculty, administrative staff, Vice-Chancellor — and yet nobody knew about them. Not officially. Security was supposed to deal with trespassers as a routine duty; but although Security was able to find and escort beyond the gates one or two individuals too befuddled or not wily enough to keep out of the way, they came back or were replaced by others. There was some kind of accommodation they had worked out within the order of the campus, some plan of interstices they had that the university didn't have; like the hours at which security patrols could be expected, there must have been other certainties we students and our learned teachers had relied on so long we did not realise that they had become useless as those red bomb-shaped fire extinguishers which, when a fire leaps out in a room, are found to have evaporated their content while hanging on the wall.

We came to recognise some of the bolder characters; or rather it was that they got to recognise us – with their street-wise judgment they knew who could be approached. For a cigarette. Not money – you obviously don't ask students for what they themselves are always short of. They would point to a wrist and ask the time, as an opener. And they must have recognised something else, too; those among us who come to a university because it's the cover where you think you can be safe from surveillance and the expectations others have of you – back to play-school days, only the sand-pit and the finger-painting are substituted by other games. The dropouts, just cruising along until the end of the academic year, sometimes joined the group down behind the grandstands, taking a turn with the zol[53] and maybe helping out with the donation of a bottle of wine now and then. Of course only we, their siblings, identified them; with their jeans bought ready-torn at the knees, and hair shaved up to a topknot, they would not have been distinguished from the younger men in the group by a passing professor dismayed at the sight of the intrusion of the campus by hobos and loafers. (An interesting point, for the English Department, that in popular terminology the whites are known as hobos and the blacks as loafers.) If student solidarity with the underdog was expressed in the wearing of ragged clothes, then the invaders' claim to be within society was made through adoption of acceptable fashionable unconventions. (I thought of putting that in my next essay for Sociology II.) There were topknots and single earrings among the younger invaders, dreadlocks, and one had long tangled blond hair snaking about his dark-stubbled face. He could even have passed for a certain junior lecturer in the Department of Political Science.

---

53 ... marijuana cigarette (Afrikaans)

So nobody said a word about these recruits from among the students, down there. Not even the Society of Christian Students, who campaigned for moral regeneration on the campus. In the meantime, 'the general situation had been brought to the notice' of Administration. The implication was that the intruders were to be requested to leave, with semantic evasion of the terms 'squatter' or 'eviction'. SUJUS (Students For Justice) held a meeting in protest against forced removal under any euphemism. ASOCS (Association of Conservative Students) sent a delegation to the Vice-Chancellor to demand that the campus be cleared of degenerates.

Then it was discovered that there were several women living among the men down there. The white woman was the familiar one who worked along the cars parked in the streets, trudging in thonged rubber sandals on swollen feet. The faces of the two black women were darkened by drink as white faces are reddened by it. The three women were seen swaying together, keeping upright on the principle of a tripod. The Feminist Forum took them food, tampons, and condoms for their protection against pregnancy and AIDS, although it was difficult to judge which was still young enough to be a sex object in need of protection; they might be merely prematurely aged by the engorged tissues puffing up their faces and the exposure of their skin to all weathers, just as, in a reverse process, pampered females look younger than they are through the effect of potions and plastic surgery.

From ASOCS came the rumour that one of the group had made obscene advances to a girl student – although she denied this in tears, *she* had offered *him* her pitta, which he had refused, mumbling "I don't eat rubbish". The Vice-Chancellor was importuned by parents who objected to their sons' and daughters' exposure to undesirables, and by Hope For The Homeless who wanted to put up tents on this territory of the over-privileged. The City Health authorities were driven off the campus by SUJUS and The Feminist Forum while the Jewish Student Congress discussed getting the Medical School to open a clinic down at the grandstands, the Islamic Student Association took a collection for the group while declaring that the area of their occupation was out of bounds to female students wearing the *chador*, and the Students Buddhist Society distributed tracts on meditation among men and women quietly sleeping in the sun with their half-jacks, discreet in brown paper packets up to the screw-top, snug beside them as hot-water bottles.

These people could have been removed by the police, of course, on a charge of vagrancy or some such, but the Vice-Chancellor, the University Council, and the Faculty Association had had too much experience of violence resulting from the presence of the police on campus to invite this again. The matter was referred back and forth. When we students returned after the Easter vacation the blond man known by his head of hair, the toothless ones, the black woman who always called out *Hullo lovey how'you* and the neat queen who would buttonhole anyone to tell of his student days in Dublin, *You kids don't know what a real university is*, were still there. Like the stray cats students (girls again) stooped to scratch behind the ears.

And then something really happened. One afternoon I thought I saw Professor Jepson in a little huddle of four or five comfortably under a tree on their fruit-box seats. Someone who looked the image of him; one of the older men, having been around the campus some months, now, was taking on some form of mimesis better suited to him than the kid-stuff garb the younger ones and the students aped from each other. Then I saw him again, and there was Dr Heimrath from Philosophy just in the act of taking a draw, next to him – if any social reject wanted a model for look-alike it would be from that Department. And I was not alone, either; the friend I was with that day saw what I did. We were the only ones who believed a student who said he had almost stepped on Bell, Senior Lecturer from Math, in the bushes with one of the three women; Bell's bald head shone a warning signal just in time. Others said they'd seen Kort wrangling with one of the men, there were always fights when the gatherings ran out of wine and went onto meths. Of course Kort had every kind of pure alcohol available to him in his domain, the science laboratories; everybody saw him, again and again, down there, it was Kort, all right, no chance of simple resemblance, and the euphoria followed by aggression that a meths concoction produces markedly increased in the open-air coterie during the following weeks. The papers Math students handed in were not returned when they were due; Bell's secretary did not connect calls to his office, day after day, telling callers he had stepped out for a moment. Jepson, Professor Jepson who not only had an international reputation as a nuclear physicist but also was revered by the student body as the one member of faculty who was always to be trusted to defend students' rights against authoritarianism, our old prof, everybody's enlightened grandfather – he walked down a corridor unbuttoned, stained, with dilated pupils that were unaware of the students who shrank back, silent, to make way.

There had been sniggers and jokes about the other faculty members, but nobody found anything to say over Professor Jepson; nothing, nothing at all. As if to smother any comment about him, rumours about others got wilder; or facts did. It was said that the Vice-Chancellor himself was seen down there, sitting round one of their trash fires; but it could have been that he was there to reason with the trespassers, to flatter them with the respect of placing himself in their company so that he could deal with the situation. Heimrath was supposed to have been with him, and Bester from Religious Studies with Franklin-Turner from English – but Franklin-Turner was hanging around there a lot, anyway, that snobbish closet drinker come out into the cold, no more fastidious ideas about race keeping him out of that mixed company, eh?

And it was no rumour that Professor Russo was going down there, now. Minerva Russo, of Classics, young, untouchable as one of those lovely creatures who can't be possessed by men, can be carried off only by a bull or penetrated only by the snowy penis-neck of a swan. We males all had understood, through her, what it means to feast with your eyes, but we never speculated about what we'd find under her clothes; further sexual awe, perhaps, a mother-of-pearl scaled tail. Russo was attracted. She sat down there and put their dirty bottle to her mouth and the black-rimmed fingernails of one of them fondled her neck. Russo heard their wheedling, brawling, booze-snagged voices calling and became a female along with the other unwashed three. We saw her scratching herself when she did still turn up – irregularly – to teach us Greek poetry. Did she share their body-lice too?

It was through her, perhaps, that real awareness of the people down there came. The revulsion and the pity; the old white woman with the suffering feet ganging up with the black ones when the men turned on the women in the paranoia of betrayal – by some mother, some string of wives or lovers half-drowned in the bottles of the past – and cursing her sisters when one of them took a last cigarette butt or hung on a man the white sister favoured; tended by the sisterhood or tending one of them when the horrors shook or a blow was received. The stink of the compost heaps they used drifted through the libraries with the reminder that higher functions might belong to us but we had to perform the lower ones just like the wretches who made us stop our noses. Shit wasn't a meaningless expletive, it was part of the hazards of the human condition. They were ugly, down there at the grandstands and under the bushes, barnacled and scaled with disease and rejection, no-one knows how you may pick it up, how it is transmitted, turning blacks grey and firing whites' faces in a furnace of exposure, taking away shame so that you beg, but leaving painful pride so that you can still rebuff, *I don't eat rubbish*, relying on violence because peace has to have shelter, but sticking together with those who threaten you because that is the only bond that's left. The shudder at it, and the freedom of it – to let go of assignments, assessments, tests of knowledge, hopes of tenure, the joy and misery of responsibility for lovers and children, money, debts. No goals and no failures. It was enviable and frightening to see them down there – Bester, Franklin-Turner, Heimrath and the others, Russo pulling herself to rights to play the goddess when she caught sight of us but too bedraggled to bring it off. Jepson, our Jepson, all that we had to believe in of the Old Guard's world, passing and not recognising us.

And then one day, they had simply disappeared. Gone. The groundsmen had swept away the broken bottles and discarded rags. The compost was doused with chemicals and spread on the campus's floral display. The Vice-Chancellor had never joined the bent backs round the zol and the bottle down there and was in his panelled office. The lines caging Heimrath's mouth in silence did not release him to ask why students gazed at him. Minerva sat before us in her special way with matched pale narrow hands placed as if one were the reflection of the other, its fingertips raised against a mirror. Jepson's old bristly sow's ear sagged patiently towards the discourse of the seminar's show-off.

From under the bushes and behind the grandstands they had gone, or someone had found a way to get rid of them overnight. But they are always with us. Just somewhere else.

2003

Visit to the Eastern Cape

Antjie Krog

The sun is already drawing water, but we still have one more visit ahead of us: Canzibe Hospital. We drive and the road is tarred. We drive and then the road turns to gravel. We drive and the road turns to stone. We drive and the road turns to ravine. We struggle across the stones, rev out of the ditches, spin out of the mud and the sun sets over the most beautiful fertile valleys in the country. There is a haze of trees. At the gate the guard stops us. While we wait for permission to enter a young woman in a light blue candlewick gown saunters past with a two-litre bottle of amasi[54] in her hand. She walks through the gate and we see on the back of her gown it says: TB.

We drive into the premises. The hospital consists of a series of small buildings in which separate units are housed. It is overgrown with the most beautiful trees reaching their branches in gigantic stretches of shade across the complex. Lower down are stands of nut and banana trees, pomegranate hedges. But everything testifies to terrible neglect. Some of the large trees have been chopped, or rather torn and hacked, down. Mildewed walls and broken windowpanes. The patients are obviously responsible for washing their own clothes, which lie draped all over the felled leaf-mould tree trunks. Everywhere there are pools of water, rubbish lies around in heaps. In front of the first building is a commemorative stone with an inscription in Afrikaans: *This hospital has been donated by the NG Church Congregation of Robertson. For the love of Christ. 1961.*

---

54 ... thick milk (isiZulu and isiXhosa)

Inside the building are four children suffering from kwashiorkor.[55] They sit with their thin legs, skinny arms and unblinking little eyes on their mothers' laps on the floor. They eat pumpkin and pap[56] and there are orange peels on a plate. One woman tells us that she has brought her four-year-old grandchild. She is looking after eight children and her husband. The mines have never paid out his pension. The only food she can provide is mielie[57] meal thinned with water and then boiled. No vegetables, no meat, no beans. Sometimes she does have money for food but lives in too remote a place to get hold of anything other than mielie meal.

There are no sheets on the beds; the maternity ward has a single blanket, no pillows, no towels. And everywhere the smell of sewage and neglect. We are fired up. We demand to see the doctor. We don't care that it is half past six. He is still on duty in the administrative section, we are told. With our list of complaints we walk up the steps, slap-bang into a short Indian man with hair sprouting from his eyebrows and a stethoscope around his neck. In broken English he invites us into his neat office. We look questioningly at one another.

"I am Doctor Kabir and I want to thank you for your noble hearts," he says while looking down at his fidgeting little hands, turning us into the complete arseholes that we are. "We have here a hundred and forty beds for a population of 169 000. We run from here eleven clinics and ten mobile points. The hospital should have five doctors, but I have been alone here for seven years. The past year two Cuban doctors have joined me, which made things a lot easier. We have an X-ray machine, but our anaesthetic machine broke down in 1998, so we can no longer do any operations here. Even caesareans have to be referred to Umtata. We have excellent nursing staff, motivated, hard-working, kind, a good dispensary with all the medicine we need and an assistant pharmacist, but not enough ad-

---

55 ... a form of malnutrition

56 ... porridge of finely ground maize meal, staple food in South Africa

57 ... maize (South African English), also *mealie*

ministrative staff. People with the administrative qualifications do not want to live here because it is so isolated."

"Why do you live here? Where did you qualify?" I ask.

"I come from Bangladesh. I worked in western Zambia for some time, then in Mozambique, then here at Canzibe. I ... " and he gives a half-hearted shrug of his shoulders, "like it here. The area is reasonably crime-free. One or two bullet wounds per month, few stab wounds. Last week some men held up the gate guards with guns and stole two of our six vehicles. We phoned Umtata and they were caught. But the bad roads make the maintenance of vehicles impossibly expensive. We usually only keep half of our fleet running."

"So these limitations do not daunt you?"

"Limitations are relative. This hospital is much better than where I worked in western Zambia. I believe that motivation comes from within and that this is all part of the challenge."

The incidence of malnutrition has gone down, he says. There was a stage when the wards were filled with kwashiorkor children. Personnel are frequently sent into the more remote areas to educate people about healthy nutrition. The women who bring their children to the hospital are also taught about nutrition. Water supply and ways of purifying water have also reduced illnesses. AIDS is a big problem, says Doctor Kabir. It is currently the number one cause of death in most hospitals in the district. In 1995 he did the different tests himself in the laboratory – one in five people were positive then. Now it is almost everyone. "You actually get a fright when someone is HIV negative." The hospital had to have a new wing added two years ago to house all the patients. The poverty in the community makes it impossible for families to look after their relatives.

"Why are there no South African doctors?"

"They don't want to work under these conditions. We had one here from the medical school in Umtata, he lasted eleven days, then he said: This is not my kind of place. Another one in the early nineties stayed for eight months."

We sit there ashamed of ourselves, not even wanting to think about all those who have left the country.

"Shall I take you to the new wing?"

A long passage stretches before us. Doctor Kabir walks ahead. He opens a door and takes us into this lonely place where death has come to stay. From the ten beds in the first ward, stick-thin arms and legs rise. Some dazedly try to lift themselves, others just flutter their fingers on the blue bedspreads, one stretches his arms out to the doctor. One person's mouth is encrusted with sores, another gurgles. The doctor opens the door across the way. Another ten beds. Heat and fever. Another. He continues down the passage, door by door, ward after ward, bed following bed, person after person, skinned into thinness, black skulls with staring unseeing eyes. The edges of their eyes welted with undignified fear.

Doctor Kabir keeps on walking. The helpless, grim anger from the male wards overflows into the female wards, becoming a complete surrender to despair. I see the woman with the two-litre amasi bottle who passed us at the gate. She sits and drinks while tears wash across her cheeks. Out of her frightened eyes still stares the wish to love. Next to her lies a woman displaying almost no sign of skin or flesh. Black bone splint there. No need for tongue. Only breath turning the ill blood over and over. And helpless, despairing eyes. Another turns her enlarged gaze towards me. Not for help, not to blame, but as if remembering herself as a woman, lovely in her bones, living her whole heart's life through days when what she loved was near at hand. Before she came to know only this darkness of flailing flesh, of falling hair. They wait like ferns to die.

This is the end of the world. And I have nothing to make sense.

And nobody and nothing, nowhere, to balm them, every one of them, carefully to lift their limbs and sop them into all that is – my lungs desperately search for a word to breathe from – apple and trellised light. To bathe their blistered tongues in song and cool vowels that fall and fill. To lay them back for the last time on a world fairer than dreams.

Doctor Kabir keeps on opening doors. I turn around and walk, and then I am running down the long passage out of these Novilon[58]-clad vaults of misery and dry death. I gasp out into a night transient with dew.

Around me the flowers have grown fangs, but I breathe.

Coldness comes paring down, but I breathe.

Only the moon. The moon showers silver across Canzibe.

And I breathe, in order not to suffocate with shame. I want to blame. I want to pluck someone from somewhere and shake him for answers. What happened to us? Where are all the dreams we once had for ourselves? What happened to our desire to change ourselves, to release ourselves into unsuffering lives, living this land more lovingly? What happened to our dreams to change the heart of rage of this country into one of care? Where are we? Have we forgotten so soon what we wanted to be?

How could we ever become what we would be, if so many parts of what we are die daily into silently stacked-away brooms of bone?

2004

---

58 ... brand of vinyl floor-covering

Unclaimed

Paul Schlapobersky

His place is the low wall on Diagonal Street, in front of the diamond building. The photographers in Joubert Park do better business because they're near the Noord Street taxi ranks and Park Station, but there's too much competition over there, and too many dangerous boys. He is busy anyway, where he sits, and people like the special photos he can do here on the edge of downtown, with the glass diamond building as a backdrop for their portraits. For the double exposures he uses old lenses; the ones that wedding photographers once used to put the bridal couple's faces onto champagne-bottle labels. First, he takes a photo of the background – usually the diamond building, or the skyline, but sometimes a Mercedes, a taxi or a soccer logo sticker – and then he changes lenses and takes the portrait, without advancing the film, to create the composite image of the face merging with the background. He also has a lens that allows mirroring of the image. That is a popular one with young men, because they can have a photo shaking hands with themselves. These are difficult, because the outstretched hand must be in the right place in the frame to create the illusion of a man greeting himself.

Mostly, though, his pictures are ordinary portraits; photos to send home or to give to boyfriends, girlfriends, husbands and wives, or to put on chests of drawers. Many are documents of the first day on the job; security guards and police in uniform, office workers in white shirts with ties, women in matching skirts and tops. People in church outfits or in traditional dress. The people are from everywhere: Zairians, Togolese, Zambians, Mozambicans and South Africans from all over the country.

His long box of photographs is organised according to the date when the photo was taken. He tells people they can come back after three days (except if it rains, because then he can't finish his film and take it to the Photomat), but some people take a long time to return, and some never come back. In the box there is space for about six months of photos and after that he takes them out of the box and leaves them at home.

Over the years the unclaimed photographs have started to take up space in the tiny bachelor flat that he shares in Berea. The man he lives with is a Togolese whose unsuppressed eccentricities impress the photographer, who himself works hard to hide his differences, to fit in as much as possible and draw no attention to himself in this hard city. The Togolese shouts at everyone in French, wears a grey suit while selling vegetables on Rockey Street, and had for a long time a tame white rabbit that sat under his stall every day, eating cabbage leaves in the shade. On the day that a crowd rampaged down the street, overturning the stalls of foreign traders, the rabbit bolted in fear from beneath the table and was killed by a car. That day the Togolese man stood in the middle of the road in his torn suit, and screamed in French at no one and everyone, and when he came home he shouted at the photographer about the amount of space the boxes take up in their small home, before curling up on his mattress, still in his suit.

The photographer is always on the verge of carrying the boxes down to the pavement below for the rubbish trucks to take away, but can never do it. The unclaimed photos are a problem; not exactly precious, but impossible to throw away. Partly, it's because they are his workmanship, but also simply because portraits of strangers, like letters written by hand – even a strange hand – are difficult to put in the rubbish bin. Though he handles hundreds of photographs a week, he still feels strange when he finds someone's picture lying on a sidewalk in the city, as if its presence there is a mistake; as if it must have been lost by accident.

One day, there was a woman who spoke the photographer's distant and rare language and who had many photographs taken in her orange dress. They had both agreed on the red-brick wall of the Reserve Bank for the backdrop of her portraits, after checking out the light at the fountain and beneath the porticos of the shops. She spoke to the photographer of the need to send these portraits home quickly, as a reminder. A reminder of what, he had asked. Had she left home so long ago that nobody would recognise her?

When she had first arrived at his low wall in the sun, it had seemed to the photographer that there was a darkness falling across each of this woman's movements and weaving itself through her clipped sentences; a heaviness and sadness hanging on her thin frame. His delight at recognising the voice of a person from home, and his natural friendliness, brought her out of her shadows momentarily, and they talked for a while of their faraway land. As soon as the photos were taken, however, she seemed to grow tired and she suddenly seemed smaller and frailer than she had a moment before. She left, and repeated his "three days" mechanically before disappearing around the corner.

She never came back for her pictures, and he realised after about a week that every day he was waiting for her to return. It was that woman who never returned whose absence disturbed the heavy silt of fear lining the bottom of him, swirling it through his being – fear of the dark things convulsing the city, of murder and car crashes and AIDS, of the wild and powerful forces that lay just beyond the frames of his innocent and optimistic pictures.

That woman's photographs eventually joined the others in his room, but on the wall next to the stove, not in a box on the floor. He looks at them sometimes, and tries to see something in them that will answer the questions he has for her. Since her, he has been weighed down by a sadness he feels every evening when he opens the door and sees the brown boxes, knowing that before he goes to bed he will have to add to them from his portable work box. He knows there are many reasons why people don't pick up their photos – they forget or run out of money. But he also knows that this city steals many of his customers away, pulling them off its streets indifferently, leaving only their unclaimed pictures.

2004

The Pebble Path

Tanya Chan-Sam

I'm not usually awake at this time. I had set the alarm for half past six because I have to be up early today, but it feels as if I've been awake every hour. I last checked the time at half past five and I've been dozing since. I turn over and see the blurred, digital figures beside me. 6:10. I can lie for a few more minutes and watch through my half-closed eyelids, how the light moves across the balcony, nudging past the steel bars welded onto my window frame, illuminating the polished parquet tile floor of my bedroom. I love watching the morning play of light percolating the darkness away, falling in big thick wedges of lemon yellow onto my duvet. The turtle doves, gathered on the electricity wires outside, are coor-cooring loudly.

Rajesh, my colleague, and I are driving out to Klein Vallei today. We're going to collect some background information for a case we're working on. I was reading through the files last night and have left them in a pile in the lounge. I mustn't forget to pick them up on the way out.

In my small kitchen, I get the milk out of the fridge, and reach under the sink for a saucepan to boil it in. I've become so addicted to that first cup of coffee that I have to have it before I can start to think straight. The bitter fragrance inside the coffee jar transports me to my childhood, when my grandfather would make *moer koffie*[59] in a tall, enamel, coffeepot. He would sit in his basket chair on the stoep,[60] looking out towards the distant mountains surrounding the farm, and sip his strong, black coffee.

---

59 ... ground coffee (Afrikaans)
60 ... veranda (Afrikaans)

I take my coffee out to the balcony and hold the mug close to my nose, so I can breathe in the steam drifting off the surface. I love that first sip. The heat of the mug against my palms contrasts the cool air on my bare arms. The mountain is cloudless today. The lower slopes changing colour from the faded russet yellows and brown bay colours of the leftover winter foliage to the fresh spring green of new shoots. I've decided to be brave and wear a sleeveless top today. It'll be hot in the car and I can feel a definite change in the air. The tree tops in the gardens below are still, because the wind has finally stopped blowing. It's been like a caged beast all week, hurtling around street corners and throwing itself against the sides of the City Bowl.

I haven't seen the local *bergies*[61] at all this week. They disappear when the Cape Doctor arrives. It was one of them who told me the wind here is called the Cape Doctor because it blows all the ills and aches of Cape Town away. In the olden days, it was the frightening, foul air of the plague that the Doctor blew out to sea, but nowadays it's the pollution and the thick smog that hangs over the city … I work on the Foreshore and it gets so muggy, you can barely think. It was like that all last week. Then, the first inkling of that wind. I know it's here when the litter starts blowing around my knees. Within hours, empty chip packets and loose newspapers are being whipped up around people's heads. And I know that on the evening news, they'll be showing someone on the Foreshore hanging onto a lamppost for dear life.

The first year I arrived in Cape Town, I walked out of the office and the wind literally lifted me up. I grabbed the nearest person and just hung on. I clung onto the flaps of this guy's jacket, and we struggled up Long Street like that, me clinging to his jacket, while he ploughed through the wind from one lamppost to the next.

The Cape Doctor's finally blown itself out to sea and today it's calm. The air seems filled with tiny particles of fizzing light and just inhaling it is making my heart beat a little faster. I don't know if

---

61 … vagrants, especially living in Cape Town (Afrikaans)

it's the coffee or the intoxicating, early morning air. I hear a knock. That'll be Rajesh.

"Hey Emelda, this is early, man." Rajesh smiles, a blaze of teeth.

It took me a while to understand his fast, clipped, Natal accent. Mine is a much slower, *plattelandse*[62] one, although here in Cape Town, I've learnt to quicken the pace of talking. I lock up and we walk to my parked car. Rajesh pokes fun at the multitude of security devices I have for my car. Immobiliser, toughened-steel steering lock, gear-lock and a sign saying, THERE ARE NO VALUABLES IN THIS CAR. He says I'm so polite informing the car thieves of the contents of my car. I just smile because Rajesh can talk, he doesn't even own a car. As I turn into Buitenkant Street, the robot[63] is red and my eyes flicker from the rear-view mirror to the side mirror and back again. I feel the cool air on my arm before I realise Rajesh has rolled down the window. A tiny stab of panic makes me say, "Just close the window, please, Rajesh."

Rajesh doesn't say anything and closes the window slowly. I wait for a gap in the streaming traffic to swing onto the highway. Rajesh is saying something about breakfast and eating, but I can't pay attention now. I have to concentrate to get into the right lane. Once I'm in the flow of traffic, I can relax. The traffic is heavy at Groote Schuur Hospital, but once we've changed lanes onto the N2, it starts to flow smoothly and it's not long before we've passed the Athlone Towers, the cardboard and tin shack settlements near the airport, and signs to Macassar and the Strand. Rajesh has taken the hint and not spoken for the last few kilometres. He's busy reading the files I brought from the office.

"Have you read these files?" he asks.

"Mmm," I answer. "I read most of the stuff last night."

"Ooh, good girl." His accent lengthens "girl" into two syllables: "ger-erl."

---

62 ... rural (Afrikaans)

63 ... traffic light (South African English)

He smiles that toothy grin again. He's nice-looking, Rajesh, as long as he doesn't smile too often. His teeth make me think of big *mieliepitte*[64] on a cob. His black hair is gelled up in short tufts. It looks very cute like that.

"So what do you think?" he says. I haven't heard his question.

"What?" I ask, swivelling my eyes to look at him quickly, before I return my gaze to the road. He turns in his seat and fixes his eyes on me. He has lovely eyes, unexpectedly light brown, the colour of deerskin.

"Why do you think Andrea Tomaso asked us to collect the statements for this case?" Rajesh repeats his question slowly and pedantically.

"Well, for one, she's an attorney and we're junior lawyers, so we do all the spade work … " I reply, equally slowly.

"I'll allow that, counsel." Rajesh says jokingly, as he pulls a mockstern face.

"Two, you're a bright spark and … " I continue, but he interrupts.

"I'll definitely allow that, counsel," he chirrups.

"Two," I repeat in a sing-song voice, "you're a bright spark who's going to help Baker, Baker and Tomaso fight their compensation claim against the Education Department."

"And?" Rajesh wags his forefinger at me.

"Three," I continue, "I can speak the right *plattelandse* Afrikaans."

"Ok, I'll allow that, counsel." He waits, then says, "Any more, counsel?"

I shake my head and chuckle. Rajesh is a lovely guy, full of wit.

"Well spoken, counsel," he continues, "but you know, Emelda, you shouldn't be so down on yourself. You're a good lawyer, heh. You should believe that."

---

64 … grains of maize (Afrikaans)

He is smiling at me when I look across at him, those teeth again sticking out beyond his lips.

"Mmm," I reply, not really knowing how to respond to his compliment.

Why do I do that? He's right. I do put myself down. A lot actually, and then I don't know how to respond when someone compliments me. I glance at him again. His light-brown eyes, circled by dark, *tamaletjie*[65]-coloured skin, look ahead.

He shifts in his seat and opens another file. We've passed Somerset West and my little red Citi Golf is beginning to climb Sir Lowry's Pass. It's chugging up around the hairpin bends in third gear. Rajesh looks up from the files and asks, "What mountain is this?"

"It's part of the Hottentots Holland, or the Gantouw, as the Khoi called it," I reply.

He turns to look at me, his eyebrows raised. "How come you know that?"

"I got a book out the library. I've always been fascinated by place names. I wanted to know," I say, shrugging my shoulders.

He turns back to the file on his knee. I look at the pass we're driving through. So different from when I was a child and my father would drive his old Corsair across this pass. We'd stop at the top and look out over False Bay. He would point out Hangklip to our left, Muizenberg in the distance and far-off Table Mountain. My sister and I used to beg him to tell us the story of how the Khoi and early Boere[66] used to cross these passes. He would describe the oxen, muscular and plodding, toiling over the rocks, the loud crack of whips, the bellows and roars of the beasts. My father's descriptions always left a lump in my throat. He made it seem so real, and I could sense his compassion for the oxen. Much like the road workers we passed on Sir Lowry's Pass in the 1960s, hacking at the mountain-side, wid-

---

65 ... South African variety of toffee

66 ... farmer (Afrikaans), used as a collective term for Afrikaners

ening the roads and tarring the mountain surface. "See these poor black men," he'd say, "they're the oxen of today."

I look at the pass in my rear-view mirror. Table Mountain is just a smudge on the skyline above the sprawl of Cape Town in the distance. I hear my mother's voice, "*Jy sal gevang word.* Don't be telling the children such stories."

She would change the subject, "Look at the daisies in the fynbos.[67] Look, there's a sugarbird flapping its tail."

I would watch the bird's long tail feathers as it hovered above the proteas,[68] see the green, spring wheat covering the hills, rising up to the blurred indigos, mauves and purples of the distant mountains.

Rajesh's voice brings me back, "I'm hungry, man, when are we stopping?"

"There's a place not far, a craft shop and café. They do breakfast there."

"Good," he says, then turns back to the files. "God, these statements are just ... how sick are these guys, man. These girls were what ... eleven ... thirteen ... here's a twelve-year-old. Kids, man, just kids," he says, flicking through the pages. "And they did it for years. And got away with it for such a long time, heh."

"Yes," I answer, letting out a long sigh, "it's tough reading, isn't it?"

We both nod silently. I feel turbulence in my chest. I had to stop reading a few times last night because my breath was brittle.

There's a car pulling out to overtake me. I watch it pass and see the sign for the café just in time. I change gear and slow down.

"Toilets, great," says Rajesh, as I pull into the car park, "see you in there."

He is out of the car before I switch off. I watch him cross the gravel car park, his dark suit flapping around his skinny body.

---

67 ... fine-leaved, shrub-like vegetation
68 ... flower species common in South Africa

It's just after nine o'clock. Rajesh finds me in the café and we order. He has the Full South African Breakfast, which comes with two eggs, bacon, boerewors,[69] tomato, cheese, fried onion, steak and half a loaf of toast. Plus coffee and juice.

"Good Lord, Rajesh, where do you put it all?"

I've ordered toast and coffee, just jam, no butter. The butter comes anyway and Rajesh slathers it all onto his toast.

Just after ten, I finally turn off the N2 and follow the signs to Klein Vallei. The road is lined with tall oak trees and begins to incline as we drive through a wooded valley. The sun is ahead of us now and back-lighting the trees. I'm passing too quickly to see, but I know the smudged haze is an artist's palette of green daubs on the branches. I slow down and lower the window. Rajesh looks at me, raises one eyebrow, and says "Careful."

"Smell that," I say. There are fruit orchards in blossom beyond the oak trees lining the road. Further up the mountain, I can see pine forests, geometrically planted. The smell of pine resin and damp earth and spring blossoms is heady. I drive slowly through the valley, breathing in the scented air.

It's just gone eleven o'clock when I drive up to the school and park near the low buildings. Through an open window, I can hear voices talking in loud tones. A man approaches us before we can unpack our files, holding out his right hand.

"I'm Eddie Pretorius, the acting principal," he introduces himself, "We spoke on the phone."

"Welcome, welcome," he repeats, "The parents are all here, all here." He clasps his hands together at his chest, his short body folding around them as if he's cold.

"Summer is nearly here, it's warmer today, isn't it?" I say, wanting to make conversation.

"Almost, almost, when the snow finally disappears off that mountain there," he points at the helmet of snow on the mountain

---

69 ... South African sausage, consisting usually of pork and beef (Afrikaans)

range enclosing the valley, "then we know spring is here, then we know."

He ushers us into the classroom and introduces the group of parents we've come to see. I look around and notice there's a single chair positioned at the teacher's table. I hesitate, unsure where to sit. I'm distracted by the classroom, so similar to the one I was taught in. The same, faded map of the world pinned on the wall, the dusty blackboard, the low sound of chalk being scribbled onto a blackboard next door, the smell of stale bread and sweat. An old knot tightens in my gut, shipwrecked feelings about canings at school, fights with friends and the isolation of being teacher's pet. I hold the files in front of my body and square my shoulders.

I turn to look at Rajesh. He is already bending his long legs to fit into a small desk, twisting around to face the parents who have seated themselves in the low, wooden school desks.

"I'll just fold myself into this desk," he jokes, manipulating himself into the seat.

Eddie Pretorius has moved the teacher's chair closer for me, and I sit down gratefully. I'm cross with myself for being distracted by my memories. I tighten my grip on the files I'm still clutching to my chest and look up at the parents in front of me. A woman sitting alone catches my attention. She has deep-set, nut-brown eyes, ringed with long, dark lashes that curl onto the circle of skin on her eyelids. "*Bok ooghare*," my mother used to say. *Goat's eyelashes.* I was never sure if she meant it as a compliment or an insult. But this woman's eyelashes are beautiful.

I'm feeling a little awkward, not sure how to start. Eddie and another teacher bring in mugs of tea on a tray and leave the room. Rajesh takes the lead and starts talking to the parents, explaining the purpose of our visit. He's offered to meet them individually, but they are in agreement that they want to do this together.

"We are in this together, we have to stand together to fight this. We want no more secrets in our community," says Willem, his lips folding awkwardly around the unfamiliar English.

The woman with the beautiful eyes, introduced as Maria, is sitting to my right. She blinks slowly, holding me in her gaze. The other parents sit behind her in a semi-circle. The men all wear jackets, poorly tailored and grubby. Maria's hands emerge from the baggy cuffs of the oversized cardigan she's wearing, as she begins to speak.

"I'm a poor woman. I'll always be a poor woman. I don't expect fantastic compensation from the Education Department," her voice falters. Her hands disappear into the sleeves of her cardigan, which envelops her, her elbows visible through the threadbare wool.

"I want them to take responsibility," Maria continues, "for someone they put here, and wouldn't take away." She stops again, her eyes brimming with tears. She wipes at her eyes and brushes her hair back with the palm of her hand.

"I was raped by that principal when I was fourteen years old," she continues, her tremulous voice holding the horror, "I never told anyone because I was scared ... scared of my father, scared my mother wouldn't believe me ... scared I would be called jags ... that I would be blamed."

She lowers her head into her hands, the middle fingers joining at a small, crescent-shaped scar on the edge of her hairline. The scar tissue curves and disappears into her head of bushy, jet-black hair like a pale woodland trail. A shaft of sunshine and the fluorescent light overhead combine to make a myriad of tiny, iridescent lights dance on the top of her bowed crown. She lifts her head and moves her hands up to her mouth, speaking slowly from behind her fingers.

"When my own daughter got raped by that man ... all I wanted was that she doesn't go through her life thinking it's her fault. That's why I want the Education Department to take responsibility."

Her fingers wipe at her moist eyelashes. My mouth opens but I don't know what to say to her. A *snik*[70] slips past my lips. I'm caught unawares by it, and glance in panic at Rajesh. His deerskin eyes have tiny moats of tears around them.

---

70 ... sob (Afrikaans)

"Maria," he's saying to her in a low voice, full of concern, "I'm so sorry. This man's abuse has been terrible for your community. We're here to get any information that'll make your case stronger."

I look back at Maria and then at the other parents behind her. Doris and Paula, two stout women, both wearing flower print dresses under navy blue tracksuit tops, place their hands on Maria's back and rub gently. They start to speak simultaneously.

"The Education Department, they knew about this man … " says Doris, her finger jabbing the desktop.

"Ja, they knew for years … " reiterates Paula, nodding at Doris.

"This is not the first time we've complained," continues Doris.

"Not the first time, we even laid a charge, *nê*?"[71] Paula looks around for confirmation as she speaks. I feel an inappropriate urge to giggle at their double act. All the parents nod their heads, looking sombre. My nervous laughter disappears down a rabbit hole and I bend my head to take notes as fast as I can.

Doris continues, "Nobody believed us. It was only when these two new teachers came, Eddie Pretorius and Sylvie Beukes … "

"Eddie and Sylvie … *regte*, *proper*, teachers," mutters Paula.

" … they had the courage to speak out. And help us to get rid of that principal. And now we are going to take the Education Department to court, because they should have done something years ago," Doris ends with a nod of finality.

"Years ago," Paula echoes.

I concentrate hard on Tomas who speaks in a broad accent, rolling his r's and tossing his head to emphasise his words. "*Ons is arme mense. Ons werk die hele dag oppie boer se plaas. Ons is dankbaar virrie skool, want hoe anders sal onse kinders leer? Hoe kan 'n skoolmeester so iets doen?*"

I nod my head while he's speaking, looking straight at him, then translate for Rajesh: "We are poor people. We work all day on the

---

71 … question tag

boer's farm. We are thankful to the school because how else would our children learn? How can a school master do something like this?"

Petrus stands up, clutching at the lapel of his mustard-striped jacket and clears his throat. The wrinkles on his forehead, like growth rings in a tree, make him old enough to be my father, but he reminds me of a nervous schoolboy.

"*Ek en my vrou,*" he reaches for the woman's hand next to him, "*ons is groot mense. Om praat'ie van seks'ie en ons is normaal. Wat gaan met onse kinders gebeur, noudat hulle eerste seks met 'n abuser is?*"

I keep translating, quietly: "Me and my wife, we're adults. We don't talk about sex. And we're normal. What's going to happen to our children who've had their first sex with an abuser?"

Rajesh and I ask questions, take notes and probe their lives for the next two hours, wanting to ensure the defence has no material to defame our witnesses. Finally we are finished, and I carry the teacher's chair back to the table. I want to talk to Maria, but I don't know how to. As I turn to join Rajesh and the parents, I notice she is at the door. Doris and Paula are on either side of her. Outside, Eddie Pretorius and Sylvie Beukes, the new deputy-principal, wait on the stoep. Eddie steps forward and shakes first my hand, then Rajesh's. Sylvie Beukes takes my outstretched hand in both hers.

"Thank you for coming, Emelda, and you, Rajesh," she says, including him in her glance.

I start to sidle towards the car. Sylvie turns to me and says, "We'd like to show you something."

"We really have to get back … " I start, but Rajesh interrupts me, bending his head towards Sylvie. "What do you want to show us?"

I have to bite my inside cheek in order not to huff. I want to leave, and I feel irritated with Rajesh, who is being all charming.

Sylvie walks ahead with Rajesh and Eddie. I follow meekly, the group of parents behind me. She walks across a small patch of grass to a low gate. Inside I can see beds of freshly-dug earth, rows of green plants with tiny bracts of first leaves on slim stalks, and a path winding around the garden.

Sylvie points at the garden and says, "This is the garden of healing the children have been planting."

Tomas points to Eddie and Sylvie, and says, "*En jy, Eddie, en jy, Sylvie, is julle wat onse kinders gesond maak.*" And you, Eddie, and you, Sylvie, it's you who are healing our children.

"*Is almal van ons, almal,*" says Eddie, waving his hands to include the parents.

It's everyone of us, everyone.

Sylvie opens the low gate and beckons us to follow her. The path is made of pearl and milky-coloured stones, punctuated by darker brown and grey river pebbles. I step onto it. My left heel gets caught in the stones, and I bend down to free it. Up close, I notice the dark pebbles form shapes. I realise they are initials. An R under my heel, a J in front of me. I swivel around on my haunches. There's an M behind me in russet-brown pebbles with liver spots on them, an S swirling under a parent's shoe.

"The children made this," Sylvie explains quietly. "It's a memorial path to acknowledge their abuse. Not to identify them, but to release them from the silence. Their initial is enough. We come and plant and weed and work on the path when they find the memories too difficult, or they can't settle in class."

I stand up and place my hand on the base of my throat, to stem the tears lodged there. I don't dare speak.

"The whole community contributes," says Eddie, "the whole community. They've brought bulbs, soil, seeds. You can find someone here most weekends. Most weekends."

Sylvie is ahead, talking to Rajesh, "Look, there'll be sunflowers here in a few weeks. And dahlias here … all the bulbs are over there. We've even got some beans, some lettuces here, tomatoes growing too."

I hover behind them, nodding as if I'm listening. I'm concentrating on breathing evenly, my bottom lip tucked under the top, blowing out shallow breaths. I smile with my teeth only when Rajesh and I at last get back into the car and drive off. He leans out of the window, waving at Eddie and Sylvie, Petrus, Tomas, and the other parents.

"What amazing people, man! Such amazing people," Rajesh says admiringly, shaking his head.

Yes, what amazing people, I nod in silent agreement. What amazing parents to have such courage to believe their children, to fight, to want to fight. I still can't speak. My breath feels splintered, jagged shards in my throat. My face feels flushed and feverish. I steer the car back along the mountain road taking us out of Klein Vallei. I'll be fine once I'm out of here. As I navigate a bend, my eye catches a flash of bright red. It's a ribbon. On a bunch of browning, faded flowers tied to a tree. It marks the spot where someone's died. In a car accident. A grieving relative came here to lay those flowers. Let the world know their loved one died. Like the garden. Where those children mark their loss. My left leg trembles and starts quivering. I push hard against the floor of the car to steady it. The tea in my stomach has curdled. My heart is palpitating, racing the oxygen through my lungs.

I see a farm gate ahead with a small muddy entrance. I make a sudden decision and swerve into the turn-off. Rajesh points at the closed farm gate. Ignoring his implied question, I blink rapidly to clear away the tears, and shift the gears into reverse. Then I swing the car back towards Klein Vallei School. Rajesh reaches across and touches my arm. "Emelda," he says softly, "are you ok?"

I can only shake my head.

I stop the car outside the school building. I hold my hand up to Rajesh, silently asking him to wait in the car. I walk down to the garden. I step onto the path and bend down to pick up a handful of dark river pebbles, to mark out a large E in the path.

2005